# TILLIYARD AND KUNTAKA

## A COMPARATIVE STYLISTIC STUDY

# TILLIYARD AND KUNTAKA

## A COMPARATIVE STYLISTIC STUDY

Dr. Hari Prasad Pandey

BHARATIYA KALA PRAKASHAN

DELHI - INDIA

*Published By:*
**C.P. Gautam**
**Bharatiya Kala Prakashan**
3611/5, Narang Colony,
Tri Nagar, Delhi-110035
Ph-7192770

●

First Edition – 1998

●

**ISBN** :- 81-86050-10-8

●

**Rs. 300.00**

*Laser Typesetting By* :–
*ISHAN COMPRINT*
G 16/14, Qutab Enclave-I, (DLF)
Gurgaon (H.R.), Ph.: 8 352412

●

*Printed At* :–
**SANTOSH OFFSET**
40, Anand Nagar, Inder Lok, Delhi-110035

# टिलियर्ड कुन्तकयोर्वक्रोक्ति सिद्धान्तस्य तुलनात्मकं शैलीवैज्ञानिकं अनुशीलनम्

भारतीयसाहित्यशास्त्रे याद्दशं वक्रोक्तिसिद्वान्तस्य विस्तृतं विवेचनं दृश्यते तादृशं पाश्चात्यसाहित्यशात्रे वक्रोक्तिसिद्धान्तस्य विस्तीर्ण विवेचनं न दृश्यते, परन्तु द्वितीयविश्वयुद्धपश्चात् प्रकाशितस्य टिलियर्डमहोदयस्य "Poetry Direct and Oblique" इत्याख्यस्य ग्रंथस्यावलोकनेन ज्ञायते यत् पाश्चात्यसाहित्यशास्त्रेऽपि वक्रोक्तेर्काचित् नूतना सरणिः पल्लविता पुष्पिता च। अस्य पुस्तकस्य प्रथमं प्रकाशनम् १९३४ तमे खीष्टाब्दें जातं परन्तु द्वितीये विश्वयुद्धे अस्याः प्रतयः लुप्ताः। १९४५ तमे खीष्टाब्दे पुनः नूतनं संशोधितं संस्करणं लोचनपथमागतम्।

पुस्तकमिदं काव्यशास्त्रस्य सैद्धान्तिकं विवेचनं प्रदर्शयति। टिलियर्डमते काव्यस्यसैद्धान्तिकं पक्षद्वयं सवभावोक्तिः वक्रोक्तिश्चेति। "Poetry Direct and Oblique" इत्यस्मिन् ग्रंथे पञ्चपरिच्छेदाः सन्ति। प्रथमे परिच्छेदे काव्यस्य वर्गीकरणं, द्वितीये परिच्छेदे अभिधा तथा वक्तव्यात्मक काव्यस्य विवेचनं तृतीये परिच्छेदे वक्रतायाः साधनानि प्रभावश्चोद्घाटितः चतुर्थे परिच्छेदे तेन वर्गीकरणमवलम्ब्य पाश्चात्यदेशे प्रकाशितस्य ग्रंथस्य विवेचनात्मकम् अध्ययनं सर्वेक्षणं च प्रदर्शितम्। पञ्चमे परिच्छेदे उपसंहाररूपेण अस्य ग्रंथस्योपयोगिता औचित्यं च निरूपितं वर्तते। टिलियर्डमहोदयेन वक्रोक्तिं द्विधा विभज्य सर्व काव्यचारुत्वं तच्छरीरेऽन्तर्भावितम्। वाच्य-वाचकधर्ममूलानामलंकाराणां शोभा, प्रतीकः बिम्बादिवादानां गूढ़रहस्यं, प्रतीयमानार्थस्य चारुत्वं सर्वमेव, बक्रोक्तिशरीरेऽन्तर्भावयन् तेन प्राचीनपरिपाटिमनुरुध्य काचित् नूतना विचार सरणिराविष्कृता।

टिलियर्ड महोदयेन प्रथमपरिच्छेदे मिल्टनद्वारा लिखितस्य तथा जॉन्सनद्वारा आलोचितस्य 'लिसीडीस शोकगीतस्य खण्डनं प्रदर्श्य वक्रोक्तेर्महत्वं प्रतिपादितम्। तन्मते काव्यं सर्वदा स्वल्पं अधिकं वा वक्रं भवति। वक्रतां विना काव्य काव्यं न संभवति। अतः नितरां अभिधात्मक काव्यस्य काव्ये स्थानमेव नास्ति। स्वल्पं वक्रं अधिकं वक्रमनर्गलमेवं। अनेनेदं प्रतिपद्यते यत् टिलियर्ड पहोदयस्य वक्रता न सामान्यवक्रता अपितु अभिधायाः कविकर्मकौशलमहिम्ना वक्रत्वं, उक्तिवैचित्र्याभावात् वक्रता चमत्कृतिं न धारयति। तन्मते अभिधात्मककाव्यस्य यद् वैचित्र्यं तत् साधारणशब्दार्थोपनिबन्धनमूलकमेव। इत्थं विविच्य तेन अभिधात्मकस्य तथा वक्तव्यकाव्यस्य विस्तृतं विवेचंनं प्रदर्शितम्। काव्यमिदं न नितरां गद्यमयं अपितु इतिवृतात्मकं तथा वर्णनात्मकं भवति। अथ काव्यमिदं प्रकारत्रयेण विभाव्यते—

१. सामान्यं वक्तव्यकाव्यम् (Simple statement)

२. अलंकृत काव्यम् (Embroidered Poetry)

३. छद्मकाव्यं (Disguised Statement)

अथ सामान्यवक्तव्यात्मककाव्यस्य प्रकारद्वयं भवति– एकं पुनर्सर्जनात्मकं काव्यं, द्वितीयं सिद्धान्तयुक्तं काव्ये एवं वक्तव्यात्मककाव्यस्य द्वितीयं प्रकारमिदं न केवलं नैतिकतां प्रदर्शयति तु—अपितु समाजस्य गति देशकालस्य परिस्थितिमपि च सूचयति। यथा ड्राइडिनकृतं 'Religio Laci' तथा जान्सनकृतं 'Vanity of Human wishes' इदं नैतिंकं अथवा सैद्धान्तिकं वक्तव्यकाव्यं प्रयोजनत्रयेण महत्त्वपूर्ण प्रायेण भवति। प्रथमं जटिलतायाः अभावेन द्वितीयं सामाजिकेन उद्देश्येन तृतीयं महान्तस्य नैतिकसत्यस्य वक्रकाव्यद्वारा समुद्घाटनेन।

वक्तव्यात्मककाव्यस्य द्वितीयः प्रकारः कस्यचिद् सिद्धान्तस्य विशदतया व्याख्यां करोति अथवा काव्याभित्यक्तेनैतिकतां स्थापयति। प्रमाणार्थं तेन ब्राउनिंग,बायरन,शेक्सपियर, विरचितस्य काव्यखण्डस्य सोदाहरणं विवेचनमपिकृतम्। तत्र टिलियर्डमहोदयस्य महदाग्रहासीत् यत्सामान्यजीवनस्य प्रतिबिम्बनमपि काव्ये महत्वपूर्णं फलं प्रदातुं शक्नोति। अतः वक्तव्य काव्यमपि तेन विभागद्वयेन विभज्य अप्रस्तुतविधानस्य महत्वं सुचितम्।

अस्य पुस्तकस्य संशोधने मम गुरुवर्याणां प्राचार्य श्री उदयन शुक्ल महाभागानां यावत् सहाय्यमपेक्षितमासीत तावत् तैः प्रदत्तम्। तेषां मार्ग दर्शनेन विना एतत् कार्य शक्यं नासीत्। राष्ट्रिय संस्कृत विद्यापीठस्य उपकुलपतिमहोदयैः पण्डितवर्यैः प्रो० वाचस्पति उपाध्याय महोदयैरपि अस्य ग्रंथस्य संशोधने आशीर्वादःप्रदत्तः। मम पितृतुल्यःसाहित्याचार्यः श्री गुणवन्तरायभट्ट महोदयेन संशोधने तथा टंकणादिकार्ये भूरि परिश्रमः कृतः। तेषां बारम्बारं अहं उपकारभारं स्मरामि। पुस्तकमिदं सहृदयरासिकाना, अध्येतृणां छात्राणां काव्यमर्मज्ञानां कृते कीदृशी उपयोगि भविष्यति इति तैः सम्यक् अवगाहनेनैव निमज्जितुं शक्तः भविष्यन्ति।

लेखकः

डॉ हरिप्रसाद पाण्डेयः

प्राध्यापकः वड़ौदा संस्कृत महाविद्यालयः

म.स. विश्वविद्यालयः बड़ौदा

भाद्रपद गणेशचतुर्थी १९९७

# CONTENTS

# FOREWORD

Forward of a book is nothing but its synopsis - a summary - a conception of what the writer wishes to convey in the entire book. It is just like squeezing sea in a ciborium - a Herculean effort to put in a pit the great Himalayas; but then there is crude method also - to give a vicarious description of the same item in a different form - in a metamorphosis - just a transmogrification of original vastness.

Two different writers - Eastern and Western - propound the same theory - of oblique expression - slanting/ironical exhibition of their views in a lucid way. It is upto the reader how it interprets and understands it. To deep thinkers, they could over it carefully, whereas super silious would just pass over cursorily and ignore it - even the original and the comparison - both.

It is just the 'meaning' that matters: The word meaning caries a vast meaning in all the respects. It carries colossal chaos and cosmos - both. Easily and un-easily each letter of the alphabet carries a meaning; every sign a symbol, a dot, a curve, carries a meaning, - such symbols and signs added to the alphabet, metamorphoses the meaning materially. Prefixes/suffices in the form of letters or pair of letters, or words, carry different meanings, according to the text, time, and place. One meaning at one place or province may not have the same meaning, at another place. If we go on giving examples of each, it would need an additional volume, which is beyond the reach of this compass. The 'meaning' differs from person to person, - what is applicable to one, may not necessarily be applicable to another - the other should have a different word altogether and not the same one - according to the meaning desired to be conveyed.

Then touching the subject of the book hereinto - there are 'direct' meanings and 'indirect' meanings - each different from one another - poles asunder - according to time, place and person. Told to some one else, applies to some one else.

When the poet describes cloud-less, calm sky, it manifests silently the subtle silent status of mind of the writer. The environmental beautification of natural surroundings, describes, how in the good mood the writer is. The oozing of Dew drops - the drizzling of showers, the fragrance - laden flowers diffusing delicate perfume in the air, all these normal situation create history.

Shakespeare,
Byron,
Shelly,
Keats,
Dryden,

for reading, understanding, digesting, one has to have a taste without which the relishing too would be a task.

When poet put down words in the mouth of character -

'Et tu Brutus'

'Frailty! Thy name is woman'

the poet does not write poetry, he create history. Years have gone by, the words to-day even are as fresh as daisy. They disperse the same scintillating sensation, what they had done in the past. Thus the irony, the oblique expression is not that of to-day-this tradition is ancient - age-old and we all relish the taste at all times. The human nature which was years ago, it is till the same to-day - without an iota of change - the same mercenary manifestations of feelings, hatred - vengeance - vices - the number of 'bads' out-wits 'good', and we still wonder how come the world, although so many years have gone by, has remained the same.

Molestation of ladies, Kidnapping of Sita by Ravana, duping Ahalya by Indra, and many more - including denudation of Draupadi in the presence of elders - all these evils - those were rampant in the days of yore, are still flourishing even this day to-day; the newpapers are full of evil news every day. The poets have written poetries, the dramastists have staged dramas, novelists have written novels, - though out the world - but the human being has remained the same - possibly has gone from bad to worse - there has been no impact of literature at all - it seems - all the labour of the learned people have gone to waste; Many many saints, sages, and good men have preached this world but to purpose.

And in this humble attempt we have tried to compare two writers with our own angle - how far they are right in their expression.

We wonder, as to far we are right ?

# PREFACE

According to the dictionary meaning - it is an introduction to book stating subject: and the meaning of the word "treatise" is 'Literary composition dealing more or less systematically with definite subject;

My handing of the subject, vis-a-vis the above two dictionary meanings is quite different - it is out of the rut - it is out of the tradition - it is fortunately abnormal. Being the student of Sanskrit language, I had a picture in my mind, as to how the ideas evolve and take a specific shape in a specic form. For example:

Signs

Symbols

Letters

Pre-fix

Suffix

Words

Meaning

| Direct | indirect | slanting |
|---|---|---|
| | comparison | oblique |

Comparison comes finally at last - after having undergone a process. A comparison may be between two equals or not equals. It is just like a photograph - it exposes - it does not pre-suppose, suppose - or impose; it shows exactly what it is And that is comparison - this is this - that is that - the questionable qualities come to the fore and put before us - the readers, what is what. Just like "Swan-Theory", we have to select the 'Milk', leaving the 'water' behind.

The book happens to deal with two ideologies; Eastern & Western - The Oriental and Occidental. What has been stated by Tilliard has been established long back by Indian authors; much much beyond, but than we cannot say - who is wrong who is right. What has been written by Shakespeare, has been written by Kalidas and what has been manifested by Tolstoy has been emphatically emphasised by Tagore - the distance of thousands miles have vanished and we just wonder as to the 'nature' as to how the nature works on the same lines - the same ideology - the same description.

The colour of the Sky, the coteries of clouds, convened in the sky, the cosmos of planets in the sky, the galaxy of flowers; the fragrance of flowers in the air - either in the east or in the west, would be all alike, enhancing, impressing, awe-inspiring under all the circumstance, and then we wonder how the nature is bountiful.

But then, the angle of vision differs - the same thing looked at by two different persons, are interpreted by both the persons, independently, in their own way and vision; the Shakespeare would look at his thing in an English atmosphere, where, the Kalidas will look at Shakuntala in Indian atmosphere/environment only. In England - in Europe - there is a system of address as 'Good Morning' - why ? Because of the fact that the environment every day differs - If there is a good morning they will have to greet it is 'good'. But then one interesting episode need be quoted here to emphasise what is being stated herein within:

Once an American visited country side in England; and his host took him around for a 'walk'. The vernal season was on and the greenery was all around and in abundance and the poetic English man could not resist himself and expressed himself in soliloquy: 'Spring in the Air' (The vernal was all around: the spring season was at its best and he just could not resist himself - control himself and the words jumped out of his mouth, automatically.)

Unfortunately, the American over-heard his expression and grumbled and shouted 'Why should I' (The English man asks him to Jump in the air and why should the American do so at the command of the former?")

To pick up the thread of conversation, we would like to stress that every meaning has a meaning:

On page 709 of the concise oxford Dictionary, the word 'Mean' has three different meanings - One as noun, two as adjective and the third as very - 'purpose, have in mind (mischief, business, to do) design, destine, for an object; intend to convey or indicate, signify, import and the word 'Meaning' has two meanings. - That what is meant, with meaning significantly and expressive, significant.

In this attempt, we have tried to simplify the 'Meaning' - how far it is direct, how far indirect, how far oblique - and we should boldly say that the comparison has been a good exercise. Both the writers are right in their own efforts - Eastern - although old and ancient, even to-day it is true and fresh, and the Western - although medival - has given full justice at his hands. We cannot just super-impose any quality of 'good' or 'bad' on either - both are equal in their own angle - in their own vision. They are at their best - they have excelled in their manifestations in the best possible way. Without casting any aspersion against any one/any thing. They have carefully analysed the situation having a grand look at the pros and cons of the problem, in their own way. They have cited several quotations, which we do not list here, for want of space and time, but any way they have done their best - all the best.

In fine, we may conclude that the slant-saying is rampant even to-day; We see the politicians washing their dirty linen in the public, their attempts to character-assasination, their oblique- language all speak of base human nature and in our efforts to evaluate the past with the present, it is better, if we would spare some words to cool porridge.

We request the valued readers to kindly point out to us - our faults - our mis-quatations - our mis-understanding, if any - at all, which we shall try to remedy in our next attempt. The suggestions too are welcome. The name and address of the author is appended in the 'Introduction of the author' and whatever your opinion is, please do not hesitate to pen it down which would throw light on the path of truth and tradition.

We are also thankful to the publishers for having thking keen interest in this humble attempt and to give this effort to put before the public in a book form - their enthusiasm and appreciation commands our regards and laurels. With a vote of thanks, we have proud privilege to bless them all.

**Ganesh Chaturthi,**
**1997**

**Dr. Hari Prasad M. Pandey**
**Baroda.**

*Chapter-I*

# Introduction

Sanskrit Literature is rich - unquestionably - no doubt; Years have gone by, Eons have gone by - the time has passed into thousands of years and yet Sanskrit Literature is as rich as ever; as fresh as ever, as relishable/ as palatable, as ever. More you study it, more you like it, more you love it. In all other subjects, at one stage or the other, you will feel a feeling of averseness, a feeling of uncomfortableness/uneaseness, whereas Sanskrit literature is the only subject, where you never get bored - you never get tired; more you taste deep, more you relish it because of its versatility, variability, veracity and virtue.

Many writers have given their views on their subjects of liking, and these views, these creations, these eternal creations are permanent, steadfast, and lasting for ever and ever. Nothing has withered them, in the past, nor the future will do so.

The Book 'Poetry Direct a Oblique' by Tilliard is worth having a second look. It deals with the principles of Kuntak manifested by him in his book "Vakrokti - Jivitam' in a very lucid way. It is an interesting study for those who are the students of the Poetry of Sanskrit Literature. "Swabhavokti" and "Vakrokti" are the aspects, which always draw attention of those who are interested in the subject. The Book of the Tilliard also touches the subject of the Book 'Dhwanyalok' written by Shree Anand Vardhan. He has taken care of both the books mentioned above; if you read between the lines, you will find that he has endeavoured very cleverly to blend the two together in his own dexttrous way. That shows his deep study of the subject too; and had it not been so, he would not have justified the subject, in the splendid way that he has done. Tilliard & Anandwardhan go parallel - the difference is in observation only. Tilliard has based his remarks/observations, having taken into consideration only western poetry and that also in short. His principle observations is based on the principle's of 'Vakrokti' only. But even in 'Abhidha' analysis, his observations is quite important. In India these principles have been discovered 1000 years before, whereas, the western learned persons have taken the responsibility on this own about having found out this principle in the 20th Century. Although the subject discussed is the same, Tilliard's observations and criticism is important and worth its weight at appropriate level. Whatever Tilliard observes, it has to be observed and compared with the Indian domination.

As far as Tilliard is concerned, his attention is towards, "Dhwanivad" only, but when he gives examples, he has been brought nearer to Shree Ramachandra Shukla. "Rasvad" (before Shuklaji) was complete in its Indian atmosphere and having its Indian technique and handling; he was supporter of the several principles beneficial to Indian culture; This is also the observation of Tilliard. He too is also having in insight of practicality and his depthness is not only imbibed with 'rasa', but also it affects 'Bhavtatva' in reality. Although he is supporter of the beneficial principles, he has considered the advise of Mathew Arnold as wrong and directed that he should select any other subject. In a poetry, subjects relating to lofty ideals must get appropriate place in literature - this he has made abundantly clear. He is opposing the theory of Arnold because it does not suit his technical thoughts which have no background. He is of the opinion that the high ideals must have a background of some personal experience with the hope of 'Dhwani', he should express himself effectively. He has put all his force in the principles of 'Dhwani' in his book.

**Classification of Poetry**

It is an observation that the western world is not fully aware of the oblique poetry, as is in occidental hemisphere. The Indian Philosophical approach to the problem is practically untouched by the westerners, in as much, as if it is raw itself; whereas as Indians have drunk deep - have had a splash & plunge in the dealing with the science compared to the other part of the world. We do not fully agree to this observation or the statement inasmuch each country, each language has its own speciality, own peculiarity, uniqueness; No doubt, Sanskrit is said to be the mother of all the languages, and many other languages derived full benefit of the richness of Sanskrit Language, and developed their own, but nevertheless, each has its own touch and taste.

Here Tilliard in his book 'Poetry - Direct and oblique' has tried to touch this subject superbly, according to his capacity, understanding and estimate; and we should admit that he has been successful in his attempt.

The Book was first published in 1934, but then due to world war all his copies were destroyed and in 1945, its new publication was taken out, with revised comments and assessment. This principally deals with the principles of poetry; He deals with the direct meaning and the oblique meaning and he is at his best in his own unique style and method and impressed the critics by his classic examples. This publication is divided into five cantos. First deals with classification of poetry, in second, it deals with the direct meaning and different forms of poetry. In the third canto, much light has been thrown on oblique poetry and its influence all around. In the fourth canto, having taken the previous canto as its base, he has tried to try his hand at the English literature and its influence, impact, etc. and in the fifth canto, he has tried to summarise by having a good observation on its classifications and necessity. The examples given in the book are from top-standard books and of popular poets. The book has been an important one because of the poetries given in the form of examples are beautiful and lovely.

**Classification**

Tilliard has began his book by criticising comments of Johanson's 'Lisides' - He has tried to denounce the criticism. Lisides is a poetry written by Milton in the form of a folk song. According to Jhonson this is a poetry which is a direct one which is not relating to mourning nor appropriate in any other form. Tilliard sees deep meaning in this poetry and he challenges Jhonson that his standard of criticism is defective. He propounds that he has kept this poetry in a wrong category and that he has not been able to look at it with appropriate angle. This is an oblique poetry and then he clears the definition of oblique poetry. But before the clarification, be admits that there is a material distance between direct and oblique poetry - it is not a full- fledged distance. Direct poetry is also a style; it is never possible to have a perfect direct poetry.

*He writes in his book that –*

"The Terms 'direct' and 'Oblique' are a false contrast. All poetry is more or less oblique, there is no direct poetry. But the terms, 'less oblique' and 'more oblique' would sound ridiculous and the only way to emphatic or even generally intelligible is by exaggeration to force a hypothetical and more convenient contrast." Page 10. He accepts direct and oblique difference by two examples. Both are showing village location. One is 'deserted Village' by Goldsmith and second is independent poet Black's 'The Echoing Green'. The Goldsmith's poetry reads as under:-

*"How often have I loitered over thy green,*
*Where humble happiness endeared each scene.*
*How often have I paused on every charm,*
*The sheltered cot, the cultivated farm,*
*The never failing broke, the busy mill,*
*The decent Church that topped the neighbouring hill,*
*The hawthorn bush, with seats beneath the shade,*
*For talking age and whispering lovers made!*
*How often have I best the coming day,*
*When toil remitting lent its turn to play,*
*And all the village train from labour free,*
*Led up their sports beneath the spreading tree*
*While many a pastime circled in the shade,*
*The young contending as the old surveyed;*
*And many a gambol frolicked o'er the ground,*
*And slights of art and feats of strength went round*
*And still as each repeated pleasure tired,*
*Succeeding sports the mirthful band inspired."*
*On this poetry the comments of Tilliard is as under:*

Here the Goldsmith has made an imagination of a village on having seen many villages and he carries the impression of those. He does not describe a real village, and hence its relation is not only with the direct meaning but also with the oblique interpretation. In actual reality it is a specimen of an original direct poetry. If the poet was specific about a particular village, he would have been more realistic. We keep this poetry in this category because this poetry does not depict any oblique meaning, but it straightway describes what is actual reality.

Undisturbed chain of words, with full freshness, describes subject, with bright sun, with strength and tranquillity. If there is non-clarity somewhere, it is only traditional word usage and not the oblique implementation. When the poet describes humble happiness, he means humble and happy people. And when he uses the words 'talking age', he mentions about the talkative 'Old age' and thus this usage is nothing but a traditional proverb and not more. It is not that the poetry is entirely oblique-lessness. According to Tilliard, Goldsmith wishes to convey that the people of a village are industrious, serious and still enjoying the life in its perfection. If there is obliqueness in this poetry, it is due to the fact that the poet does not tell the tale directly, but through the medium of a village, he describes an image of a human nature through poetry. With the happy medium of this explanation, he wishes to describe that the old happiness always turns into fresh happiness and with the help of the poetical license, he would like to re-creat his day-dreams into sectional reality. It is to be noted that Shree Ramachandra Shukla also says the same thing; although he is supporter of direct poetry, he too believes that poetry is a reflection of the poet's mind. Out of this reflective meaning, if there appears any other meaning, Tilliard gives it a symbolic terminology of oblique poetry. To give an example, Tilliard has quoted the following poetry to clarify his stand on oblique poetry.

*"The Echoing Green"*
*The Sun does arise,*
*and make happy the skies;*
*The merry bells ring*
*To welcome the spring;*
*The skylark and thrush,*
*The birds of the bush*
*Singh louder around*
*To the bells cheerful sound.*
*While our sports shall be seen*
*on the echoing Green.*

*Old John, with white hair,*
*Does laugh away care*
*Sitting under the oak,*

*Among the old folk*
*They laugh at our play,*
*and soon all they say,*
*"Such such were the joys*
*When we all, girls and boys,*
*In our youth time were seen*
*On the Echoing green.*

*Till the little ones, weary,*
*No more can be merry;*
*The sun does descend.*
*And our sports have an end,*
*Round th laps of their mothers,*
*Many Sisters and brothers,*
*Like birds in their nest,*
*Are ready for rest,*
*And sport no more seen*
*On the darkening Green.*

In this poetry, we can have the complete oblique poetry which is in the poetry of Goldsmith. The description of beauty is definitely the best, but yet this a beautiful example of an oblique poetry. It is not the aim of the poet to beautify the scenery. According to Tilliard, this is a more serious form of poetry, then expected and the spirit is that in fulfilling any body's wish, there is a pleasure. There is no desire in this poetry, but the main theme is that of pleasure only. The nature fulfills its daily routine in a beautiful way, old John experiences a perfect sense of full satisfaction, little children play playfully well and get ready for rest and in fine, the singing Greenery turns into darkened greenery, because its work is over. The beauty also indicates this very idea. This poetry depicts a feeling of a ripe apple which just falls on the ground at smallest touch.

The meaning of this poetry is not direct anywhere. Every sentences is a separate entity and yet it is presented in a totality form. Hence in comparison with 'Deserted Village', it is quite different from it. It is full of oblique approach.

Tilliard is of the opinion that wherever a poetry, free from oblique approach, when it describes the professed subject directly, it can be said to be a 'direct Poetry'. Whereas when a poetry tries to indicate something else, other than the one specified in the poetry, it takes a form of a oblique poetry, its rays manifest not the original meaning, but a twisted, different meaning, a different tune altogether. Thus it depends on the poetry, to which it tilts - whether it gives a direct meaning, meaning nothing else but a direct approach to the professed subject, but then when it suggests indirectly other than the subject discussed, in the garb of examples, it takes a form of 'in-direct" poetry, which is nothing else but an oblique approach to the subject.

*Chapter-II*

# Direct Poetry / Direct Saying

Tilliard has classified one class of poetry as a "Direct Poetry"' or a 'direct statement'. We can call it a descriptive form. Because it is so, it becomes very near to narrative formation. But then it cannot be classified as such. There is some difference between the two. The seeds could be traced from time immemorial. Even after 'Fishing' or even by a terrific incident, one realises to resort to pleasure by and from the poetic creation. Hence it cannot be prose nor it is modern. The poetry can be divided into three categories:

1. Simple Statement Poetry.
2. Reinforced and Embroidered Poetry.
3. Disguised statement.

The simple statement has two types of divisions. One is a creative poetry and second is a poetry composed of some statement or justiciable sayings. The first type is that which relates to some incident or event, which takes place normally, and when the writer arranges them in his pen in order to describe that event, a prose description takes place. The reader is interesting in its reading because the arrangement is not that of the writer's own, but it can be associated with any one, at any time, at any place. On page 18 Tilliard says that –

The kind which deals primarily with an actual happening either physical or mental, which gets its value for author through ordering the happening and which is relevant to the reader because happening and its ordering are not just private to the author but could occur at any time or place and to any normal person. Tilliard has specifically mentioned three examples in this regard.

1. Milton's' poetry written on his 23rd birth-day.
2. The Tower by Yeats.
3. 34th Chapter of Meriden's Book 'The Modern Love"

By giving all these three examples, he wants to assert that except the professed subject, these do not give any indication towards any other meaning. 'Jhansi Ki Rani' by Smt. Subhadra- Kumari Chauhan is an eminent example in this regard.

On Page 18 Tilliard manifests that 'There is a second and copious kind of direct poetry that does not refer to any actual experience but expounds a doctrine or expresses general moral ideas.

According to the intensity of the experience, the poetry has its own level. Some are written by extreme deep feeling of experience just as Drydin's 'Religious Laici' or 'Vanity of Human Wishes' by Jhonson. Whereas in some the level of experience is quite low compared to reader's expectation. For example 'Confession Amantis' by Goer - which he has given in full length and established that, there is some oblique-ness here and there, but yet it is a description of a 'miser' which has been well brought out by the poet with a planning. The entire description is a manifesto of a principle of the society that one who collects the money, may not, cannot be the owner of the money. He is a collector only.

This ethically or principally motivated poetry is having three phases. First, it is void of complications and it gives a clear picture of the mental aptitude and due to that is becomes more important in the eyes of poetical structure due to its serenity and grace. In this, we keep a straight eye on the subject itself - not through an intermediary and when we are not in the mind of reading a grave subject, we read only simple composition. Meaning to say the individuality of the writing is in itself its speciality number one.

Secondly this poetry is associated with a specific social element. The greatest truth is always exhibited with the help of oblique poetry only. Whereas direct poetry is always useful for little social problems to be tackled and it is always useful as such.

On Page 22, he writes that "But the small social and moral commonplaces, the more quotation of human passions pass easily into direct statement."

To confirm his statement, the writer has discussed the sayings of Browning, Bayran, letters on 17th Century, and Shakespeare. Many of the Shakespeare's poetry are of this type. Shakespeare's statement that the 'all the world is a stage' is not a truth, which is universal, but it is only an experience, which any one of us can feel and experience. Many moral truth are derived from such poetry. The third point of this poetry is that this being a middle class poetry, it is helpful to us in finding out the parameter for a higher class of poetry. The greatness of Chauser, or Goer's simplicity, or Milton's magnanimity, or Tennyson's lucidity is related to this phase only. Here Tilliard quotes Poet. He clarifies about an Epic/Lyric and such lengthy poetry in this perspective. Each lengthy poetry is a series of a small and honest poetry, which is tied with the string of length to whom, we cannot call a poetry. Thus the ordinary poetry remains un- attended; but Tilliard is positive that we should accept the necessity of ordinary poetry and we should enjoy the pleasure, which we derive out of it.

In the second category of direct poetry, there are two divisions; One reinforced direct poetry or 2. Ornamental poetry. When rhyme/rhythm or ornamentation do not do anything except decorating, even then, the direct poetry is poetry only. When the tune, or a statement which is unconcerned, and mentions something else, then the oblique poetry starts. Real decorative poetry is only a straight poetry - it cannot be said as oblique poetry, because it does not contain any suggestive meaning. In a descriptive poetry, anything can appear.

When the subject of description is clear, then it can be said that it gets strength from repetition or when ornamental description is there, it can be said to be ornamental poetry.

In the matter of giving more strength to the style, Tilliard gives more stress on onomatopoeia. On account of more use of this, there has been severe criticism of this usage, but both of them are extremist view-points. One of the critic has compared Dryden's poetry with Virgil's 'The Aneid' and supported that a poetry with maximum use of onomatopoeia too can be a very good poetry. In Sanskrit such poetry is called 'third grade' poetry, but still it has its own charm and impressiveness. The onomatopoeitic poetry has its own magniticism and versatility. The alteration not only touches the core of the subject, but it touches the soul too and makes it a reinforced poetry and not only that but also sometimes, it is capable of oblique creation also suggesting altogether a different angle of the subject. Dryden's following poetry is an example of meaningful suggestion, but except that it does not lead to any oblique indication;

"The trumpets loud Clonger Excites us to Arms With shrill Notes of Anger and mortal Alarms The double double double beat of the thundering Drum, Cryes, heark the foes come; charge, charge," its too late to retreat.

It has sufficient onomatopoeiatic rhythm - it is a best example of direct meaning. There is obliqueness in this poetry, as much is needed in a good poetry, but when it sounds over and above and intelligent meaning, the poetry becomes oblique category. For example Virgil's 'The Aneid' - 6th canto - the following lines - can be quoted which gives description of the final funeral ceremony at the time of Misenus, when wood is cut: Itur in antiqual silvam, stabula alta ferarum; procumbunt piceae; sanaicta securibus ilex; fraxieaeque trabes cuneis et fissile robur scinditur; advolunt ingentes montibus ornos.

"They travelled through those old forests that these were the right places for the game of 'hide & seek'; the leaves were scattered/stewn all over; Oak trees were being cut with a sonorous sound; or these trees were being cut with the help of axes; they were being falled down the hills through 'ash'" trees.

Here the Virgil has very aptly described the falling noise of the trees, crushing noise of axes with a hand of an expert in his art. The second line echoes the sound aptly. But just like Dryden, this poetry does not give only a description of the jungle and its situation, but it also suggests/indicates the danger of the wild animals hidden in the jungle; this is an oblique approach to the problem. There are spots of heat on the top of the tree, and it also gives an idea of onomatopeia 100%. It will not be out of place to mention here that Tilliard has in his next can to referred to the danger through oblique reference and the rhyme as an instrument to achieve the goal. But he has also stressed the point here that the onomatopeia which supports the main theme of description, comes into the category of direct poetry only and which do not suggest or sound obliqueness, it can be termed as unmixed onomatopeia. This he considers as a routine, But still in the descriptive narration, which is limited to the extent of referred subject only, he does not deny simultaneous existence of unusual high caliber and possible exhaultedness. If the subject referred to is great, or the style of the poetry is quite strong, and it supports fully the described subject, even, then under the circumstances, the descriptive poetry too can be good and great. In support of his statement, he has mentioned a poetry known as 'Loss the terrible' written by Willian Black to Buts by means of a letter. He states that in absence of any supporting meaning, it is still a good poetry and a good effort at it.

In order to clarify the decorated poetry, Tilliard has compared two poems from 'The Oxford Book of English verse" - one is 'The glories of our Blood and state" by Shirley and the other 'Ask me no more where Jove bestows' by Carew. One - the first is a principled poetry, whereas the second is a love poem. First is full of Ornamentation and the second is without. But Shirley's poetry decorates the body only by subjective approach, where as the second one, it its state of decoration-less-ness, indicates/suggests something oblique, and it comes under the category of Oblique poetry. Shirle's poetry is as under:

The glories of our blood and state
are shadows, not substantial things.
There is no armdour against fate,
Death lays his icy hands on kings;

Scepter and Crown
Must tumble down
And in the dust be equal made,
With the poor crooked sickle and spade.

Some men with swords may reap the field
And plant fresh laurels where they kill;
But their strong nerves at last must yield;
They tame but one another still;

Early or late
They stoop to fate,
And must give up their murmuring breath,
When they pale Captives creep to death.

The Garlands wither on your brow,
Then boast no more your mighty deeds,
Upon Death's purple Alter now,
See where the Victor-victim bleeds.
Your heads must come
to the cold Tomb;
Only the actions of the just
Smell sweet and blossom in their dust.

We do not elaborate further or give or offer our any comments over this poetry, because the purport is very clear.

Still however, an observation is a must: Some people till the fields with Swards, or/and they kill people also there. And there they erect now gardens, but ultimately his powerfull air surrender themselves. They look after one another, but quickly or slowly, they have to bend down before the fate, and when they are in the hands of fate, these emaciated people slip towards the death and their breathing noise come to a stop.

On your head the garlands are life-less and then don't boast about your brave deeds. Look towards the alter of death, where the blood of the victor and the defeated flow equally. Your head will be shoved under the cold sepulchre. Only the just deeds will give their flavour and will grow flowers in the dust.

Shirle's this poetry is full of morality, in which the sober gravity of death has been accepted with pride and forever. With very able dexterity, the post has woven this, though in a very lucid and thoughtful manner. Each comparison keeps it a own importance and it helps in confirming the original principle in a beautiful manner. The opposite ideas have been woven in a beautiful way to make the main idea a step of strength and ability. Its live or delicate observation leads the imagination to a new avenue and its reason gets strength thereby. Considering all these elements, even then this is a direct descriptive poetry and not an oblique one. Every couplet is having a rhyme, and still this very formation makes the principle strong-it does not indicate any irony or satire.

For example, Shailey's 'Ailester' is a specimen of a combination of both the 'ornamental Poetry' and the 'oblique Poetry', in as much, it touches both the aspects of the poetry. Tilliard has touched his lines from 67 to 128 and he discussed in detail that its beginning is showing the oblique poetry and still direct poetry is also evident. And hence this is a mixed specimen of a poetry. By giving this example of "Ailester", Tilliard wishes to emphasise the point that a complete poetry may not be always full of oblique approach of the times. One part may be with it, whereas the other part could be without it - the oblique poetry.

Tilliard has also referred to third variation, which he has branded as disguised statement. By referring this, he hints at that poetry, which with the help of ornamentation, tries to create an impression of a different poetry, but virtually it is not so - it appears to be one, where as, actually, it is the other - not the one presumed.

He writes that- 'It is perfectly legitimate for statement to dress itself up even to an high pitch of elaboration provided it does not pretend to be oblique. But it has no business to masquerade obliquity. When statement commits this crime, I call it disguised statement (p. 32).

In European literature, Malarme has given sufficient strength on the fact, the poetry must have ornamentation. And hence this pretense came into existence. In the 17th Century, there are many examples of this type; but also it has been exhibited by the modern poets also. 'Mistress' by Kadley, there are many examples of this type. Tilliard has given an example of 'separation'. 'Jorention' by 'Eliet', Ezra Pound's many poetries, and 'Huge Selwayn Maubereley' are the examples of this sort of treatment. There are many examples of this type and we here give a specimen of 'Ezra Pound' - the poetry is very clear:

*'His true Penelope was Flaubert,*
*He fished by obstinate isles,*
*Observed the elegance of circes hair,*
*Rather than the mottoes on sundials,*
*Unaffected by the march of events,*
*He passed from men's memory in lan trentionsme,*
*De son age, the case presents,*
*No adjunct to the Muses' diadem.*

This poetry by Ezra Pound is quite ostentatious. The poet has tried to decorate this poetry by means of literary reference and unnecessary usage of words to ornamentalise, but still this effort has been fruitless. The poet has failed to achieve the pinnacle of perfection, which she has tried in vain effortlessly. This sort of ornamentalization and its translation given a shock to bring it down to a low level, which gives a shock to the reader. The quotation - 'l' an trentiesme de son eage (the principle inscribed on the face of the sun) exhibits that the time has no control - it gives no other indication. This lime tries to refer to the literary style, and it does not do anything else other than that. This line refers to a ruffian and vagabond named "Willian'" who always used to sit in the cate-teria, and yet he was successful poet.

Here Mrs. Pound wants to prove herself quite the oposite. Although in the literary sense, it is oblique poetry - about which Tilliard has already mentioned about it here after, but yet in the opinion of the Tilliard, this is mostly prose order. This poetry does not expose the complete meaning and it is definitely a specimen of an ostantatious quality poetry. This is only an effort to show off as a poetical genius. In Hindi language, in Riti Alankar-Sadhana, many examples of this type could be produced - where there is nothing to be told only an exposition of one's art.

Hence, we can come to the conclusion that all the poetries, which describes real or imaginary incident and creates a phantasy, when it describes some social principle or ethical tenat, or it strengthens the subject with the help of ornamental exposition or onomatopoiatic manifestation, or in disguise describes oblique poetry, it becomes a direct poetry with direct meaning and approach. It is however imperative that the professed subject is made to strengthen and it indicates the subtle meaning but does not give any oblique interpretation.

*Chapter III*

# Obliqueness

## (Vakrata)

Tilliard has ably criticised both the types of poetry - 'Abhidhatmak' - direct and 'Vaktavya' - oblique by giving ample examples and samples. This criticism has again been divided into two sections - (1) Area of obliqueness and (2) Instrumentation of obliqueness. By area of obliqueness, he means these meanings which words over and above oblique meaning, gives other dimensions. Or by instrumentation obliqueness, he means, his approach towards the style which helps giving us different meanings. In other words, we can say that by area he means the tone of the meaning of the words, by instrumentality, he means the technique which helps giving us oblique meaning.

### (1) The field of obliqueness

The field of obliqueness covers all the poetry, which sounds irony in its meaning. Thus it covers all the vast field, without any exception. We can count on the elements of obliqueness, but as far as its field is concerned, it can be considered as a vast one only - it pervades all the poetical compositions. When a poet wants to describe any subject, he can take resort of the obliqueness and he can give a piece of his mind, by means of his art and craft. Tilliard is alive towards the difficulties, and he translates the oblique meaning under different heading; but he gives these headings as specimen only. He is of the opinion that the deep meaning of the poetry cannot be embodied in the headings only; and as such when one reads on the poetry, then only he comes across the beauty and subtlety of the poetry - the full depth cannot be judged only by heading. What he means by this, how he has dared take this decision, can be seen only in the next chapters, when we come across them. Here we shall discuss those fields, which he has tried to cover up in this thesis. He has divided obliqueness into three fields -

(1) Sensibility
(2) The Great Common places
(3) The Primitive.

**Sensibility**

Let us take up this topic now.

According to Tilliard, by describing a particular subject, the writer wishes to cover up the subject by arousing the memory of the readers. He has discussed the topic of Onomatopeia, which helps awakening the memory of the subject and by the deft instrumentation our feelings/senses are aroused. It awakes scintillates our senses. it may arouse our feelings and creates sensitivity. this sensibility can be ascribed as live sentiments. Tilliard raises the question that 'every poet is very sentimental compared to ordinary human being, then why take resort to oblique poetry unnecessarily. He himself has solved this problem in two matters. He (the poet) touches the mental standard of the ordinary human being with the help of this medium and makes him taste and understand the beauty of his creation and composition. Secondly the fact is that no poem has any outstanding quality in itself, and its absence cannot be a cause for the centre of the poet, and yet there are various poets, who are mainly touchy and they use this medium to touch the heart of the reader, through the medium of oblique poetry, when it becomes subject to criticism.

In the 18th and 19th Century, this was used to its maximum extent. When we say that this standard was misused, there is no objection. Many poems of Shakespeare, e.g. 'Venus & Adonis', Tennyson's nature-description, Pope' 'Rape of the lock', and the poems by Drumand and full of this quality. Tomsons 'Seasons' can also be called this type of poem - a lengthy poetry. Afterwards this method had to face severe criticism afterwards. The main reason was this that afterwards it was described by means of its qualities. However Shailey, who is himself an independent fundamentalist, he presented the poetry in the form of its qualities sounded by the poetry.

The simplicity of this system, gave birth to such pseudo poets that tied to follow this pattern and tried to make a scene by which they would appear to be more intelligent.

Tilliard has given several examples about the sensitiveness of the obliqueness; main are two - Geraint and Enid by Tennyson and

'Rape of the Lock' by Pope - first there five and next are six lines - these are :

*So thro' the green gloom of the wood they past,*
*And issuing under open heaven's beheld*
*A little town with towers, upon a rock,*
*and close beneath, a meadow gemlike chased*
*In the brown wild, and mowers mowing in it.*

This is completely a fantasy - a pen picture. Some call it that is has influence of pre-raffalite culture. It is a description of a city in the air, which given a reflection of beautiful hills and the cutters of the corns, which has no bearing with the real life. This is not from memory, but is is only a poetical imagination irrelevant with the facts of life. But it gives a picture of a mental state, which has some bearing with the mental state of a person. According to Tilliard, this delicate sensitiveness is the only quality of an oblique poetry. Tilliard says that the sensitiveness is the foundation of the oblique poetry and it depicts a true picture of the poet's mind.

Still this a subject of an Oblique poetry. In the obliqueness of the poetry, we shall have to see that it touches the subtle sensitiveness - whether in reality, it gives a suggestion or not, because there is no dirth of pseudo poets, who with the help of their peculiar fantastic style, they present their direct poetry as oblique one. At the time of valuing an oblique poem, we shall have to be alert towards the sensitiveness of the people who are extremely opposing this phenomena in their own defiant peculiar manner.

### The Great Pre-sumptions/Commonplace

Over and above the sensitiveness, the second field of oblique poetry is about the great presumptions. Tilliard has raised the point about the great expectations, their forms, it position in the poem and usefulness, it tune, and psychological impact on the poem and utility of the criticism.

Aristotal has translated 'terror' as a follow up of fear and compassion and after that the critics have not thought whether this follow-up is a means or an end. Almost everybody has accepted the fact that in a poetry passion is the representative of the means. Dryden too believes in this very principle. He believes that a drama reflects human beings" passion, happiness, and change of the fate in the real form. Mathew Arnold has too the same belief. Those human tendencies which are great and reflects original love feelings, which touches original ideology with a powerful presentation - and which is beyond the time limit - can be translated as interpreted as the aim of permanent literature. These human tendencies have their own feelings of joy and happiness, and simultaneously it presents the poet's art by its presentation and style. When the poetry was defined as such, in the language of beauty and pleasure, the efforts of the critics were applied towards exhibition of poetical exposition of mental faculties psychological exposition. On the strength of the psychological approach critics tried to go deep into the depth and in this effort they narrated such incidents and events, which had nothing to do with the original composition. Tilliard has no soft corner for this and still he does not reject this that whatever has been narrated in the poetry in the form of individual character with the help of which research can be made on the psychological approach to the problem. According to him, this should be done, but the criticism does not end here. The original question stands out that whether this affliction and psychological tendencies are the final achievements in itself or it sounds some different meaning seriously. The poet gives its passion a live characteristic of the writer or these passion has been pen-picture, or its existence has no less a value than its creation. Is it sufficient to know that Othello is full of jealousy and he demands acceptance or does it refer to any other meaning other than it exposes ? If we compare "Aurora Leigh" with 'Paradise Lost'; or 'Much ado about nothing' and 'the way of the world' with Browning's 'Men and Women', then compared to other authors, we may be able to find out a different meaning altogether.

This very meaning is 'Great Commonplace'. More Tilliard desires to manifest that if the passions-pen-picture is the medium, then it comes into the category of a narration only or otherwise if there is any other meaning/a suggestion, then it becomes an oblique poetry and its vastness of the meaning, a commonplace placing.

But yet these great commonplace is quite different from the narrative precept. Preaching of tenets of morality are always under the state, cult or religion but the place of great commonplace takes place the form of complete humanity. These great commonplace have been controlled and it has very good connection with the cultural history and human belongs. It is a subject of the entire human race, and it is possible that it may have been narrated only in the form of poetry only. 'Essay on Man', 'Church Porch'- these poetries, and the writings of Martin Luether and Wilhemina, cannot come under these theory, because they are in the form of a narrative style; The great commonplace cannot come under this category, because, each poetry is a specimen of a peculiar style and system. We can experience this only when we mix ourselves with the great commonplace. Just like poetry on morality, it is not in the form of a dry and chiding medium, it comes in the form of an affection and it has the basis of psychological existence and it has its foundation on the earth, there is no chance for any questioning. Its completeness makes it completely dependable. at the time of experience, the reader is under an existence of 'trance', which touches his heart/soul and mind.

> *"The great commonplace in poetry when obliquely exposed, issues from the various parts of the poem, it is that in which many experience culminate. And one cannot of course separate the value of a great commonplace from the value of all the complicated experience that go to creating or rediscovering it."*
>
> *(Page 16)*

A poetry which suggests the great commonplace is definitely a great composition, which is interwoven with the experience which one has in one's daily core. It is possible that there may be difference in the measurement of experience and ideal, but when the writer or reader reaches a stage of involvement, at that stage, the ideal and the experiment become one and it faces them both individually and one gets lost in dreams and ideology. In reality the great commonplace cannot be translated in the meaningful words, because its source is far away and its history is to varied that its narration does not leave any impression and the person who describes such series does not earn our confidence. Our confidence on him can be impressed on him only when he with his wide and varied experience which is based on the brain and heart's proof giving faculties. Generally it so happens that he leaves half the things untold so that the reader can himself experience the beauty of impossibilities and contradictions.

These Great Commonplace are very important from different angles. First of all it has its moral value. In a human being's life, many ideals come one after another. It is a big thing to translate the value of life in the poetry every time. One side the poetry faces with the modern problems, whereas he has a background of years of ancient principles and problems and between the two conflicts he tries to survive with great difficulty.

> *"In the world's history a great commonplace is every now and then brought forth, and poetry may be concerned in its birth, but those that already exist must be kept alive. They are in perpetual danger of perishing. They have to be refelt continually and reformulated by human experience. They cease to be true unless continually ratified by fresh expression. It is one of the functions of poetry, the most intense form of speech, to keep these commonplace alive, in contemporary idiom through the ages."*
>
> *(Page 43)*

The Great Commonplace has its importance because of its concentrate value. Longiness in his book 'The high value of Poetry" has written that - if the subject is of high quality, the style itself has a bearing of high caliber in it. Tilliard has in his writings accepted this principle. When a great poetry accepts some great commonplace as its oblique manifestation, it leads towards an exhaulted and serious approach. Each angle of the poetry carries a weight and on one side it goes towards valued suggestion and on the second side it leads to greatness, glamour, and towards the pinnacle of glory. The Great Commonplace is always pervading in the poetry and it does not stop at a particular place and hence it provides a great emphasis to the quality. "The Echoing Green" 'Illiad' 'Promethus Unbound' 'Lycidas" and 'Miless Tale' are so many examples of these type which support the original statement.

> *On making his observations on the great Commonplace, Tilliard has raised the question of commentary also. When we know that a particular poetry describes a particular commonplace, then the work of criticism is not over till we do not clarify the meaning thereof: "It has been decided that the poem or play is oblique, criticism of the 'Passions' should take a subordinate place and the main task should be to answer the question of what the obliquity is."*
>
> *(Page 41)*

In this connection, he quotes an example of spencer's 'The Fairy Queen;, which has been commented by Hazlit. This example of the 'The Fairy Queen' opens up with the best classical music, but yet Hazlit is not satisfied with it, because it does not suggest the meaning thereof which is concealed in the original poetry. To translate the comparatives or to comment on the tune and tone or to specialise on the insignificant facts is not a complete criticism Tilliard himself clarifies the real meaning thereof; He states that the 'Fairy Queen' by Spencer which creates a scene of heaven, and on the other side he gives a contrast of the society's structure of the world and on the third side, he would like to give a pen picture of an ideal life, which is quite different from the reality and it shows an escapism and does not desire that the picture which he would like to present would be an unreal one.

Over and above the 'Fairy Queen', he has tried to give examples of other writers also and their meaning; and he has clarified an event from 'Ilian;, where Pream asks Echailis to hand over the cadaver of Hector - this observation is simply beautiful and tasteful and as such we would like to quote it here under: This is in the last canto of 'Iliad', where Echailis has killed Pream's loving son Hector, and when he pulls the dead body on the walls of Toy, while using an absusive language. Hector had killed the loving son of Echailis, Petrocleus was very angry on Echalis. Pream was also loving his son Hector to a very great extent. Although the war of Troy was definitely a great one and hence Echalis and Pream were enemies at daggers drawn; echalis over and above this, had killed many sons of Pream, and as such this enemity had grown to a great extent. Pream was loving his son Hector so much that he went to Echalis to ask for the dead body of his son Hector. There was bitter enmity between the two - both had lost their sons - and they knew the value of the pain of son's death intently, because both had lost their sons, and each one realised the feelings of the other. Ultimately the dead body of the Hector was handed over to him. Thus 'Iliad' can be commented upon from different angle by different people. Those who are interested in excitement, they will get the best description in this. When the old dilapidated Pream Kneels at the feet of Echalis, when he kisses the hand of Echalis - this scene is such a heart-rending tragic scene, which has been created due to the killings of sons of both the parties, that it leaves an indelible impression on the minds of the readers. On this occasion the psychological mental impression of the mind of Echalis, is real, actual and true on the evil of the experience. One who reads this, develops faith in Homer and in his deep study of human nature and tendencies. To create an impressive scene, and the description of the mental state of the character, - these are the achievements of the writer in all its perspectives. Over and above the direct meaning, it has also oblique angle also. This oblique meaning is the great commonplace, which reaches the mental stages of human beings, which ultimately unite human beings - it is diametrically opposite to the tendencies, which might separate two parties. In the time of Homer, when the tendency was to fight to the finish only, and to precipitate the principle of reconciliation in those days of yore, it is really a powerful pen only which would idealise the principle of sanity, direct approach to the problem and away from the tension of the traditional enimositical environmental exigencies of those days. The handling of the human problem has been such delicately handled and touched that it exposes the deeper layer of the heart's exhaltation with a different angle- its approach is not only humane but appealing too;Due to great commonplace that human achievements have been arrived at, that its value is limit-less. Its nature appears to be religious, moral and that of another world, as if quite separate from ordinary human approach and in its climax this commonplace manifests the christian principle, which is of great value and importance that - One who saves one's life, loses it, and one who loses it, wins it. this certainly a great phenomena; with great march and environmental principle of human approach to every problem howsoever difficult it may be - the writer excels at it. Tilliard's approach to the great commonplace is an example of expression of principles which has been accepted by the people with open heart and open arms - it has reached first place and not second. According to him great commonplace can be achieved by the instrumentation of the art of expression and the art and life becomes one ultimately and does not remain separate entities. At the time of clearing the great commonplace, from the pulpit, he separates the poetry from the value and testifies the value of the art this is the intention of his advocating obliquity.

**Primitive Tendencies**

The great Commonplace is the outcome of deep thinking, dimension of the society, and the tendency of the public welfare. It is the result of the awakening of the human being. But then there are still tendencies in a human being, which can be classified as primitive, which were in existence then and even now, these tendencies are lurking alround, in one form or the other. In the poetry, these are shown as oblique tendencies. The main one is that of 'danger'. In good old days, when men had not controlled these tendencies, it was at its great height in those days. The idea of doom's day is the result of this tendency only. this is prominent in all the religions of the world. But now the society has come over this tendency on account of education and awakening, and this tendency is getting less and less. It cannot be said that it has been completely lost - simply it can be said to have been hidden or covered to a certain extent.

The second tendency of human being is that of 'pleasure'. Although the idea of new innovation is of late only, its beginning can be said to be right from 17th century. But a human being to control the science, the environment and the nature, and to get rid of the fear of 'danger', man is always working on that line only. He has been successful in his efforts and this is very clear from the successful tendencies which they have arrived at to-day; the root of which lies hundreds of years before. On account of the achievements of science these days, on account of usefulness, on account of the result of the research they have made, but yet it is very much in existence to-day, which was already there, hithertofore - a tendency of pleasure and happiness.

There are some tendencies, which create a murmur in literature and they offer a subject for oblique interpretation of life. In the literature this tendency of unhappiness appears because of its love towards past, in the form of escapism in cognito. But this is the tendency of a poet, who accept unhappiness but they cannot recognise it. Meaning to say they cannot adjust towards the situation - they cannot accept/reject unhappiness; nor they can reject unhappiness/pleasure - both. They just reject the pleasure, which is the root of unhappiness. The poet who accepts this situation of inviting unhappiness, becomes the root cause of happiness afterwards. This is a dilemma; a difficult mental outcome - a situation out of which it is very difficult for a poet to get out and enjoy the neat 'pleasure' or neat' unhappiness.

Lyrical poetry impresses us most because of its expression of sentiments in a very ordinary routine form. These exhibition of human feelings were quietly woven in the folk-songs but since the people have forgotten these ancient folk-songs, the hunger of the poets have increased. In those days the folk songs were public property and people used to satisfy themselves with the help of these compositions. Even to-day the importance of folk-songs has not been lessened. Poets like Shakespeare becomes helpless to sing folk song, when the King Lear gets involved into sentiments and sings folk songs.

Tilliard has given four examples of the oblique compositions - one of which is vergil's 'The Aneid'. One is a Children's song in French, one is a piece from Shailey, and the last is form T. Elliot. Here we give below an example of Virgil's 'The Aneid':

In 'the Aneid', Virgil has in the last lines described the battle at its height and has described the death of Turns at the hands of Anias. These lines are full of fear, which represents oblique meaning. In the battle, he has tried to turn the mind of Terms through the instrumentality of Jupiter. Jupiter sends a Fury to change the mind of Turns. In the description of Fury, the description by Virgil is very powerful it excels in the sentimental expression. When Fury reaches the earth, it turns into a small sparrow which flies over the domes of the buildings, and it moves/flies around the Turnes in a peculiar manner.

*On account of fear, his arms becomes numb. The poem reads:*
*Postquam acies videt Iliaces atque agmina Tarni,*
*Alitis in parvev subitam collecta figuram.*
*Quae quondam inbustis out culminibus desertis,*
*nocte sedeus serum cannot importuna per umbras,*
*have versa in caciem Turni se pestis of ora,*
*fertque referetque senans, elipeumque everbeasat alis*
*Olli membra novus sovit formidine torpor.*

The meaning of this is: –

"When it sees the rows of soldiers of Elian, and the troops of turns, suddenly it turns into a small arrow, which generally at night hides in the domes or on the dilapidated buildings, or with its shrill cry feels the darkness which embarrasses and in this change this cry and this flying affected Turns often and the wings dashed against his armour often. At that time ar unimaginable impact weakened his arms, without any reason.

On account of the magic to make a soldier immobile and having created him inactive, to infuse him with fear is quite impressive; it reflects the weakness of human being against fear; It is clear from the conversation between Turnes and Enias, that this fear is out of place.

Although the field of primitive tendencies is not quite clear, still however, its expression and opening for human beings is quite valuable. The poetry expresses the sentiments and this is manifested only by oblique expression mainly. It is doubtful in any other form or expression except oblique involvement.

*Chapter IV*

# Instruments of Obliquity

Tilliard has described the definitions about Obliqueness. Simultaneously he has also tried to explain the procedure to arrive at oblique interpretation. In other words, over and above the subject matter relating to the Poetry, there is some specific procedure which is dependent on the expression of oblique poetry. In order to resort to this method, he stressrs that there is necessity of the following five principles:

1. Rhythm/Rhyme
2. Symbol.
3. Reference to context
4. Oblique story
5. Characterization

Tilliard while elaborating on these points he would like to make it clear, how difficult it is when one principle unknowingly over-shadows the other. Any set example cannot be specifically shadowed only under one principle. Because it is possible that the example given may involve one or more principle together to make the meaning more effective and at that time it becomes difficult to singly categorize one from the other. While arriving at the meaning of an example, it may be possible that it would carry more than one principle and at that time, the analysis would be difficult. Thus the rules cannot be applied firmly on point. He is giving an example of a poem written by Caitles to lesbia, and by elaborate explanation, he tries to make it clear that when the subject for description gives oblique interpretation; in it there is a combination of two principles viz. rhythm and unity. The first line of this poem is 'Vivamus, mea Lesbia atque amemus'. In this the word 'Lesbia' is in the centre and this word is sand wiched between two powerful words 'mea' and 'atque' and after that only the two words "Vivemus" and "amemus" appear. Having placed the word 'Lesbia' in this peculiar position, the poet wishes to stress the point that life and love are balanced in themselves;

they move around Lesbia and if Lesbia is removed from the context, the words would be of no value. This oblique meaning is due to the strong position it carries. The utility of rhyme and unity are so combined that it cannot be incorporated in the five principles mentioned hereinabove.

It is a matter to be noted that Tilliard has not counted the unity of obliqueness, but yet this poetry has been given as an example. By doing so, he simply wishes to manifest that in order to bring obliqueness in a poetry, there are many ways to perform, but they cannot be counted. Some new poet may devise new avenue to express themselves, but that too is also not sure. Hence only five principles can be enumerated, which are mainly connected with this.

## RHYTHM / RHYME

The main principle so oblique expression is its oblique rhyme. In rhyme it creates all the impressions, tunes, and expressions of the words they carry. In the 19th century, this method was praised a lot, but in to-day's atmosphere, there is much aversion to it, then it is necessary. But generally it is an accepted fact that the rhyme plays an important role in bringing the mind on the right track. Rhyme is oblique when it describes the subject matter in an elevated form and manner and does a lot more. As it is told in the past, the rhyme helps the subject, it instigates, then the poetry becomes a Reinforced Statement and not under oblique category. Oblique rhyme, over and above impressing the subject, it relates to unrelated irony also. In the matter of example of this, the writer has commented upon the style of Vyat which is styled as Petrachijing style written with title 'If in the world there be more woe'. This poetry creates sentimental sensation. He says that there may not be other qualities in this poetry, but the sentimentalism is at the top. In the poetry 'The Aneid', when in the sea of Pelinras' the fear, which is fit for that incident and event, has been picturised more and in its original form. With the help of rhyme the definition of the entire incident has been amply made clear. Shailey in his 'Hymn of Pan' has expanded his pangs of feelings in words with his suggestive suggestions to such a deep extent, that it passes our comprehension. How much obliqueness has been dumped, how nice the criticism has been elaborately done by Tilliard. Here we give the specimen of his writing.

'Hymn of Pan' by Shailey that the poet has turned the tune

in such a way that it has crossed the limit of obliqueness. Pan has been shown as apollo's opponent at the mount of Molas before the God Molas and the description is picturesque. In this poetry he has put power of his pen into music and he has attracted the listeners, fairies, and by describing this he has shown his excellence in music and the lines are given as under :-

I sang of the dancing stars,
I sang of the draeded Earth,

And of Heaven-and the giant wars,
and Love, and death, and Birth -
And then I charged my pipings -

Singing how down the wale of Meenalus
I pursued a maiden and claped a reed,

Gods and men, we are all deluded thus!
It breaks in our bosom and then we blee

All wept, as I think both ye now would
If envy or age had not frozen your blood,

At the sorrow of my sweet pipings.

In the third line yet is addressed to Apollo and Molas and in the 2nd line below envy is related to Apollo and age is related to Molus.

The foregoing poetry is the last word of the poetry. In all the previous narration, there is a beautiful world of pleasure and happiness and in the sixth line of every poetry, the writer has used the tune of "Anapaestic trimeter" just like 'The wind in the reeds and the rushes. But in the last poetry, the poet in his line "singing how down the vale of Maenalu's, the poet is using 'Iambic Pentameter' and he has changed the tune of the poetry. Although the change appears to be insignificant, but yet the poet has been successful in creating the impression, which he wants to create. Although the lines after this, from 7 to 12, all the lines are similar - in the same tune - but here in the 6th line, he has changed the tune of the poetry. The subject of description is full if pleasure to pain and there is a simultaneous change in the rhyme and this has made a good impact reversible and it is impressive and powerful. But here the main question is that whether this change fattens the subject and whether it is suggestive of something more than the indicated. Whether in the change in the rhyme, there is impact of obliqueness. Here the subject has changed from bravery to love-less-ness. The Fairy named Syrink rejects the love and is turned into "Nersal" and due to this 'Pan' has to suffer bleeding.

Tilliard says that in this reversal the obliqueness of love is unparallel and it cannot be compared with any love poetry of the world. But this rhyme reversal shows that oblique interpretation where the human beings and the god get lost - this is not limited to the field of love. Here the poet over and above the expressed feelings wishes to show the original reality of feelings.

Tilliard has shown three examples of rhyme - obliqueness and on the strength of them, it can be concluded that whenever the rhyme touches the original subject, the rhyme will not be oblique. But when the rhyme instead of touching the original subject, draws our attention to a different tendency, and creates a different situation, the rhyme could be said to be oblique. In other words, when the original subject is by-passed and it touches other subject or interpretation, the rhyme could be said to be oblique.

**Symbolic System**

Over and over the 'Rhyme', Tilliard has also defined a small but very important 'Symbolic System' He has used the word 'Symbol' not the wide sense as is done by Yeats, but he has used it in a limited context. In the two essays 'Ideas of Good and Evil'- Yeats has covered all the elements of poetry in the symbolic system. He says that 'All art is not mere story-telling, or mere portraiture is symbolic and has the purpose of those symbolic talismans which medieval magicians made with complex colours, and forms, and bade their patients ponder over daily, and guard with holy secrecy, for it entagles in examples colours and forms, a part of the Divine Essence."

But according to Tilliard, this experiment makes the word unclear. He would like to use this word in that sense which would create a symbolic interpretation in total. In order to clear this, he compares the two poetries one that of Bern with the Black 'The Sick Rose'. Both the poetries are as under:

> *"The white moon is setting behind the white wave. And time is setting with me, O!"*
>
> *-Burns.*

*"O Rose, thou are sick!*
*The invisible worm*
*That tlies in the night*
*In the howling storm,*
*Has found out the bed,*
*Of crimson joy,*
*And his dark secret love*
*Does the life destroy -"*

*-Blake*

Yeates has written about both these quotations that both are completely symbolic. The whiteness of the Moon and the waves have bearing on whiteness; but with a thoughful angle, it has not anything to do with the evening sunset, but if the whiteness is removed from the these lines, the beauty is annihilated. But when the whiteness of the moon and the waves, and the passing of time, and suggested painful shriek of soul - if all are combined together, it creates such a symbolical combination of colour, beauty and suggestions. Tilliard comments upon the yeates this definition and comments that this cannot be interpreted as oblique poetry. There is some reason for this that the writer in the symbolic system tries to give a specific meaning of what he says, In this context the white moon has a passing phase only. It is not the intention of the poet to incorporate it any live sentiment. But definitely the 'White Moon' is some thing more than the existing moon and its exaggeration is not within - it depends on other elements also. If 'White moon' is separated from the context, it has no independent meaning - it bears no importance then. If we compare this poetry with the blake's - then 'O Rose, thou are sick' is not a poetry; it requires different context, but still the sick rose carries a weight which is not separate from burns' 'White Moon'. 'Now it is precisely this isolation that gives symbolism one of its peculiar functions (Page 64) Hence the poetry - the lines of the burns can be classified as 'narrative poetry' and not in the category of 'Oblique-Poetry.'

Opposite to this, the above-mentioned poetry of Burns is in it self an oblique-poetry. It shows the delicacy of the Rose, which is an emblem of pure love.

The insect is the bad tendency hidden in one's self, and it grows daily. Due to this the worldly love gets polluted. Here the polluted love and the sick rose comparison cannot be limited to an ornamental or oblique poem. This suggests something more than the subject. The first line humanises the Rose flower. This creates pressure on the innerself of one, and it arises our silent sensitiveness and it is concentrated on the sick rose. Although the lines ahead cool down our enthusiasm and astonishment, but by this our sentiment is more concentration on the first line only with considerable pressure and when we once know the symbolical interpretation between the real rose and imaginary rose, it creates a feeling of astonishment. 'The Line - They bed of crimson joy' is very meaningful - it does not relate only to the physical rose but it gives an indication towards the bed, where one can feel pleasure and love entwined. The whole poem draws our attention to the fact that the rose which is sick, it is an emblem of innocent love and it is the gist of the whole poetry.

Here Tilliard is alert towards one principle and it is that - whether when a poetry draws your attention to only two words of the poetry, does it restrict the vastness of the poetry ? In reply to this question, he himself clarifies that also and although the two words only are symbolically centres our attention, but its real aim is to stress the poem's force more wide and elaborate. Any word, if properly handled, has many manifestations, many interpretations, many meanings; but when this word is used in a special mode and manner, it becomes so small and subtle that it does not leave its impact over all and many suggestions crop up out of it and it widens the vista - the area - the arena. The tendency of the symbol has no bearing on its main point. Similarly the symbol, of its very nature rising out of rather than mingling with its context, encourages an expansion of though and association (Page 65) To clarify his comment, he criticises again on the poetry of Black, that if we try to find out the similarity between the love and the rose, it refers to the exclusive beauty of the chicks of the feminine form, when Burn's poetry 'White Moon' does not indicate any sort of such interpretation.

Tilliard says that vastness of the symbol, hastens to help the obliqueness of the poetry. To arrange for or to ask for a special effect from the symbolical expression is indeed a difficult effort - it is a difficult process - but yet once we have established the correct symbol, the poetry is filled with many subtle/oblique interpretations. Each symbol in a poetry is full of many oblique meanings. Hence when it is used often, then the meaning of each reference carries many more other interpretations, which may be direct or oblique. This repetition of the symbol brings many references simultaneously, but then it gives birth to a different trend and style. A reader can interpret the meaning according to symbol and it gives strength to the poetry. In this connection, Tilliard has made comments on Black's Panther, Goat, wet-coast and such like symbols. He says that the result obtained from the usage of symbols creates a specific sobriety and sincerity in its interpretation. As for example, he has discussed Illiat's 'West Land', but he is not satisfied with Yeat's symbolic manifestations/suggestions. Once a symbol is used at a particular place or circumstance, and subsequently if it is not clarified as it should be, it creates a hazy and unclear interpretation. Yeat's in his two poetries, he has used Baignetium as a Permanent symbol of intelligence, but then henceforward, there is no indication of this symbol and hence the readers are skeptical about the getting hold of the meaning of the composition. But that does not mean that the excessive use of the symbols makes a failure of the poetry. Any symbol used excessively, loses its charm, and loses its interpretation, and it becomes a mechanical and compact indication and in the hands of unskilled writers, it creates obliqueness which are full of faults. A judicious use of symbol with its powerful background creates a small but impressive get up in expressing oblique interpretation.

Tilliard says that - 'Similarly the symbol, of its very nature arising out of rather than mingling with its context, encourages an expansion of thought and Association. (Page 65)

**Un related Reference**

Over and above the Rhyme and Symbol, there is one more important item which in literary language called un-related reference from literature only. This indication is automatically and unconsciously inter-woven by the poet in his composition, when he unknowingly connects incidents and events of other poets in his own compositions - this is done purely from the memory and it will have to be admitted that appropriate change is made according to circumstances. This helps in the formation just as the symbol - system helps the poet - this can be called reference from the literature gives a steady base to the writer, and it takes its shape in the literature when it is copied from the known world literature which is quite famous. Sometimes such reference may not necessarily be literature bone; it may be from falk-tales or tell-tales. All reference to literature is an indication towards the gorgeous listed literature, which increases the beauty of the composition. For example Yeats has started his poetry 'Sailing of Byzantium' thus -

'That is no country for old men. The young in one another's arms, bird in the trees,

*- those dying generation - at the song..."*
*In these lines, yeats has referred to Keats'*
*'Ode to a Nightingale' - relating to following:*
*'Thou was not born for death, immortal Bird !*
*No hungry generations tread thee down.'*

Keats has deep faith towards his life, and hence he thinks about the immortality of a human being. His faith towards life has given birth to this poetry. And hence in his poetry 'Ode to Nightingale' - reference is a relative sensitiveness and the poem appears to be beautiful on account of its oblique quality. There is no word which has a direct meaning.

Everything has been expressed through obliquity. By this reference there is birth of combination quality and the strength of the plot.

In this way such references unknowingly even increases the beauty of the poetry; but then sometimes the poet creates such situation knowingly even to give the strength to his pen. For example Milton's 'Paradise Lost' has described the attraction of Adams' attraction towards 'Eve' - this description has a direct bearing on 'Iliad', where in the 14th canto Jeuge has been attracted towards Heir - the sounding may be incidental, co-incidental, conscious or unconscious. In the 9th Canto of 'Paradise Lost' Adam shares with the Eve the fruit of forbidden free and he concludes his proposal in the following words:

*"For never did they Beauty since the day,*
*I saw thee first and wedded thee, adorn's*
*With all perfections, so inflame my sense*
*With ardour to enjoy thee, fairer now*
*Than ever, bountie of this vertious Tree."*

Here Milton refers to the 14th Canto of 'Iliad'. The scene is - Geuge in the Trojan War gives promise to win the war and hence

Hera becomes nervous and she wishes to enchant Geuge to entrap him in her beautiful trap and wishes that he would go to sleep so that he can change his decision. With the help of Aphrodite she becomes successful in her attempt. Geuge surrenders before Hera and she says that 'so far there was no one in my heart who could be my ideal idol and her love - love towards never attracted me towards her as much your love and affection has stopped me.

The comparison of both the events is not similar. Homer has written his lines in and at the time of a happy event, whereas Milton has written at the time of unhappiness. If there is any similarity between the two is only the appreciation of a woman. But Tilliard is commenting on Milton's Iliad as under: There is some obliqueness in the statement. Even if there is a fall or a defeat, I compose my best creation, my subject is extraordinary, but I know where I am, I am alive to creation of a marathon poetry.

Here is another example. At the end of "Second Georgic', Virgil has praised the village life and his attraction towards Music is in the following lines:

*"Me vero primum dulcs ante omnia Musae,*
*quarum sacra faro ingenti percussus a more, accipiant."*

"It is true that my first and foremost wish is that I am the appreciator of Muses and I am impressed with her love and let she may accept me."

Virgil's above-mentioned version has been commented upon, in his blind description, as under:

*"Yet not the more*
*Cease I do wander where the Muses Haunt,*
*Clear spring, or shadle Grove, or Sunnine Hill,*
*Smit with the love of sacred song."*

Muses, who is afflicted with love songs of Spring, Green Groves and the sunny forests, and where she is roaming freely - please do not stop me from going there. Regarding Milton's reference to this non-related literature reference, we reproduce below the comments of Tilliard - as it is -

1. Percussus amore; smit with the love; There can be no doubt about the reference. And the effect is prodigious. Occurring,

as both passages do, in contexts of the highest poetic intensity, they are like the two extremities of a flash of lightening, sports united by a blinding stream of electric fluid. In the common love of their are the two great poets as it were mingle their minds, each gaining sustenance from the other. In plainer prose, we feel Milton's context to be enriched through the reference and we trust Virgil's lines the more because they have animated the later poet. (Page 71)

2. Allusion then is an oblique statement of 'I am writing in the tradition, I am civilised, I know what I am about, I am in touch with a civilised audience, when I can count on to understand me. (Page 69)

Generally such reference to the literature draws us - takes us to the known sources of the literature. But then there are some references which are not known to the people well, and as such they escape from the eyes of a common reader. This unclear reference gives an idea about the vast reading of the poet and if it is not so, it can be made clear that the writer has a lack of background of deep knowledge and studies and that his reference leads to ordinary workmanship. As far as the poetry is concerned, thus the transgression of both the limits - the knowledge and of - want of knowledge - are both harmful. When some reference is too close; too popular, it loses its charm and a reference to such reference does not lead anywhere - it does not increase the beauty of the composition or literature. And on the second side, there is just the opposite : The references made, howsoever good they may be, but if it escapes the notice of the reader, it loses it charm and it does not impress the reader; There is no fault of any one - it is just an appreciation of fact.

However, such references depend upon the limits of studies made. There was a time, when to be called a literate, one has had to study a particular Branch of literature in all its aspects, the deep study and going through of important books was a must. But in to-day's perspective the field of knowledge has been vast. The measurement of literature is effective and such type of reference are not favourable and yet we get many examples of this sort. The beginning of the Illiat's 'The Waste Land' indicates towards chaucer's 'Canterbury

Tale' and 'Yeats' 'Two songs form a play' refers to Shelley's 'Helas' - Another athevse shall rise'. In the poetry of Illiat we get many references about Gottier's. It is true that the plot of humor as depicted Gotiars is not fit for Illiat and generally ordinary readers may not have read Gotiars and yet Illiat openly refers to these references.

## FABLE

As far as obliqueness is concerned, the main instrument is the obliqueness of the Fable. Right from the time of Aristotal, fable - the story - is supposed to be the main synonym. To-day the fable - this word - is used to interpret planning and unison. Right from one line to many incidents are connected with this word. Katalas has written to Lesbia in which the first line is the miracle of this composition. And Arnold Banet's 'The Old Wives Tale' - such a big manifestation comes under this 'fable' only.

At the time of Aristotal the importance was given to the story only. After that Hoars became such a big poet that he maintained that the story is the main thing. But these days this importance has been withdrawn - the story or the fable is not given the importance as it appears to be and out side beauty. Planning in the too much form makes the story dull. The obliqueness of the story starts where, rhyme, symbol, language and sentiment and like are present in this best form. When other forms are present, the obliqueness stands out and it becomes more powerful and in its absence, it becomes powerless. Many times it becomes taste- less and becomes mechanical.

In the absence of a sentimental feeling, any normal brain can create a story, but in the state of sentimental existence, the purpose, the performance, the presentation becomes all the more difficult.

Fable Poetry mainly does three performance First of all it gives a picture of the greatness of the poet's mind and his patience. As has been told in the past, without the sentimental exhibition, the narration becomes life-less. The story becomes live only when the human feelings worm up to express themselves forcefully, and on the second side the brain tries to control the passion by justifying incidents and events and becomes active towards its expression exhibition. Due to the successful efforts, one would come to know about the greatness and control of the writer. The poetry - the fable - the story is the medium of expressing obliqueness and great expectations. For Example the scene of 'Iliad', when Echalis had been approached by Pream for the dead body of his son Hector, and when Echalis accepts the request, it expresses great expectations. There are two different elements - one tries to divide the two, whereas the other tries to join the two and in between the two the later is more powerful than the former, due to its inordinate 'Spring of Bandusian' by Horace.

'Miller's tale' by Chaucer, 'Lycidas' by Milton have been selected as large poetries. In these definitions, there is too much of tussle - more than when it is necessary. And it is not necessary that we should agree with all the points. But looking at the criticism, we can judge what he tries to indicate, and which can be accepted with open mind. Because Tilliard has opposed the criticism of Jhonson which he has written on 'Lycidas' - he has started his books with this only. Here we shall take into consideration the definition of Lycidas and the obliqueness of the effort made in this direction.

Tilliard has commented upon Lycidas on the obliqueness of the story and he has tried to draw our attention to the three points quoted here-in-above. First of all he says that the readers should be ready for the possibility of any third oblique interpretation and its possibilities - leaving aside Jhonson's criticism. The poetry describes the death of the friend but there is something more than that.

The second point he discusses is that before composing lycidas, Milton had travelled a lot and collected a lot of experience and having feared that the death is nearing him, he wanted to complete his work as soon as possible. This poetry expressing sorrow has been written under the mental stress he has undergone. The third point he would like to discuss is that at the time of obliqueness of the story of the Lycidas,it is also necessary to discuss other points also. Having taken into consideration all these three points, in the background, he discusses about the obliqueness of the Lycidas.

At the time of giving his opinion on the obliqueness of Milton on Lycidas, Tilliard, has also taken into consideration, the metal state of the writer and in this way at the time of writing about the death of King Edward, he has tried to find out the vast meaning behind it. Lycidas is divided into six cantos. Before the beginning and the end, there are four large cantos. Tillard says that in the beginning in the Preface when the writer describes the death of the king Edward, he - the writer - experiences his own death and the cruel fate which has played a severe part with him. The oblique meaning of this poetry is the possible death of the writer and his fear thereof, which is literally penned down in this poetry. In these 24 lines, and in between the lines Nos. 25 to 84, in the 2nd chapter, through the death of the Lycidas, he describes the world's misery, helplessness and complications all around. He expects that Lycidas should not have died. The fairies should have saved him, but they could do nothing against fate. Mues was a goddess, but yet she could not save her son Officials. In the happenings all around, we find Milton's own self-experience. He is of the opinion that if there is going to be failure, why all these efforts should be undertaken at all. At this time, there is a voice of god from heaven that the fruit of all these is not on the earth but only in heaven. - 'Of so much fame in Heaven expect they need.' The second chapter closes here. But at the end, Milton, after making a slight change in the rhyme, he is making the voice of god, fruitless. He is not satisfied with the voice of god from heaven. He wishes to stress that the events of the world and the impact there of are beyond reason. In anticipation of the facilities available in heaven, we can not define the ill-irrelevant incidents of the world nor we can obtain any happiness or peace out of that.

Having read the lines of the third canto in the beginning one feels that after a long time of patience, the writer has started his pen; These lines are:

*O Fountain Arethuse, and thou honour'd flood,*
*smooth-sliding Minicius, crowned with vocal reeds*
*That strain I heard was of a higher mood.*

Here the poet returns back to the field of sorrow and death, after dissolving the voice of god from heaven. This canto makes the uneasiness and clamour more strong than the former one. This canto is full of the world's torture, blow of fate on human beings, torturing questions the expressions full of boiling passions. Unbelievable of incidents and faults which are fought loudly, he does not hear the voice of heaven and this canto closes with the unclear future smooth-saying of Milton. These two cantos are full of contradictions; It gets developed with motion and the second one is larger than the former. But both rise from the same direction and they both fall flat on the same bank. Having reached here, we expect that there would be some settlement, but instead we get a beautiful change - a transformation in the poetry. In the next lines, after having the two cantos furious atmosphere, we now come across absolutely clear and calm surroundings:

> *Return Alpheus, the dread voice is past,*
> *That shrukks thy streams, Return sicilian muse,*
> *And call the vales, and bid them hither cast*
> *Their Bels, and Flourets of a thousand hues.*

The lines bring us to love and sweet old memories of Arcadia shifting the stand from painful mental agoney-ful status. This change with the help of obliqueness of the poetry indicates towards escapism from the helpful circumstances the situation has created. But this is only an indication and it is not real and correct settlement. If Milton had presented this as a final settlement, then definitely it would have been an unpalatable and unwelcome happening. This is only an indication. This is a situation of the poetry in the middle. It has helped to collect the experiences so far. By this the vista of the poetry has been widened and we still wish there would be some helpful settlement.

In the fifth Canto, Milton tells the farmers not to weep any more. His this saying is an indication towards the world's baseless reasoning and the defects, and it is an awakening towards the short comings and it is an exposure of his own views and ideas. Here the Milton says that Lisides, when he dies he gets freedom from the worldly tyings up, but this is the mental state of Milton towards the difficulties of the world and this is an oblique presentation of the facts.

It the last canto, the poet has created an atmosphere of peace and tranquillity with the help of oblique rhyme. This peace is not that of idleness, but it is a creation of a balanced mind, a peace of firm decision. The last eight lines of Paradise leads us to deep peaceful atmosphere and it refers to unrelated literature Illusion, by which he has pronounced the beauty of oblique structure.

On the strength of the foregoing, we can certainly say that the example of Lycidas is not that easy as is with other poetries. In reality, the obliqueness of the plot has led us to a great thoughtfulness or it has helped express a powerful brain in opening up his generous thoughts in oblique manner. Any plot can ascribe oblique interpretation and this plot of Lycidas is an example there of. This plot involves all the incidents/events together. It deals with the disturbed state of mind and the control thereon, shows poet's capacity of oblique control and his entry in the sphere of romance and ancient atmosphere is the proof of the fact that his experience is wide and varied and he is quite at ease with the different feelings of sentiments and the results thereof. The greatest thing about this poetry is that it makes us at home with the great expectations. This is not only due to the plot, other wise its greatness would be through the atmosphere of obliqueness and through plot only. It is different.

The end of the poetry is with that firm decision that the poet will go on doing his own duties in the best possible way, may he have to face to greatest difficulties in his path; he may get the result or not. He completely controls the fear pervading his mind. In fine, each reader will definitely admit the efforts of the poet about the great expectations he has in mind. There may be some hesitation in accepting the situation, because in reality, his interpretation is different. This is exhibted in the full form in its oblique presentation. In fact this great expectation manifests the beauty of christian culture that one who lets go his life for others, he really lives his life. If we accept the poetry in this light, we can confirm that 'Self- Honesty is more powerful than any other expectations of the world.' Without worrying for the result of efforts, to keep busy in one's own duty, is the summum bonum of life. In the Book 'Bhagvad Gita' by Lord Krishna, this very version is given in Sanskrit Language - that you have the right to do your duties, and that you have no right to expect the fruit thereof. This very expectation is expressed in the Lycidas in its oblique form. It is very important that this obliqueness in the poetry is the soul thereof. Tilliard considers lycidas as a great poetry. In the beginning he has indicated three points, which are beautifully and completely incorporated in this work of the poet.

**Character-Sketch**

Tilliard has mentioned this as the last and final resort for the expression of obliqueness is the character-sketch. He tries to establish the fact that one cannot detach the character from the main plot and then evaluate him, from the main plot, where he is the main character in the whole plot. Whatever the poet wishes to express, he can do so under this very scheme and not out side. There is no separate entity for the character outside the plot. He admits that the Greek philosophers puts more stress on 'fate', and it does not leave any gap for the expansion of psychological aggrandisement but the writings of Shakespeare and his characterisation gives full justice to the character-sketch and it is a first step forward towards the art of expression. Ebson also falls in the same category but excessive psychological treatment has set down several measures which are defective by themselves. They have started evaluating the characters separately keeping them aside from the main plot. For example, Shelley's 'Promethus Unbound' - its criticism and comparison of Promethus with Satan. He further says that to separate Promethus and Satan separately - this procedure is full of faults. It is true that the characters play an important part in establishing ideas of the poet - they are helpful in that way. But this can be true only when one considers that the characters are completely united with the main plot of the story.

When a poet tries to immortalise his characters, it is an established fact that by and through the medium of the characters, he tries to express his own views through the medium of oblique expression - say indirect expression. In that case the characters become only symbol of the society. They may be the instruments and not the goal. They are the forms of some great expectations and not the translation of the thoughts. They themselves are ideas and thoughts. 'Wife of Bath' by Chaucer is an example of this characterisation.

It is the belief of Tilliard that in any composition, the story is the main instrument through the help of which, great expectations are expressed obliquely, but at the end of the chapter he admits the truth that in any composition, the characters sketch is the principle obliqueness. In this connection in the field of prose literature, Dickens 'Pickwick Papers' have been defined well. These are not borrowed characters. His creation is natural, but still then, it has become a medium of oblique expression. He does not leave even once an opportunity, where he cannot get an experience. He is full of anxiety and enthusiasm. He always wants to see others happy. His simplicity and his tendency to trust others has gone far from the real world.

Out of his character, there is exposition of three specialities in an oblique manner. First is that he gives and ideal form to his thoughts, Secondly he teaches to love the neighbours and third he gives an eternal form of childlikeness. It would be improper to say that he represents children. the children learn from experiences but Pickwick does not learn from that. In this way the character of Pickwick is repeated in the process of progress and hence the character of Pickwick has become an emblem of Obliqueness in a greater form. This proves that the plot is made secondary and the characterisation of the characters is made main.

Tillard on Page 67 writes that -

The Evolution of Pickwick way thus go to prove that, in spite of Promethus and Satan as interpreted above, a character may be the main obliquity in a book and dwarf the plot in importance, and that one should not allow recent predilections for plot-pattern to rule out that possibility."

Thus Tilliard has defined Rhyme, Symbolism, un-related literature reference, plot/story and characterisation in his book. But still he has made it clear that there may be many ways for oblique- expression and yet these five mentioned herein above, are main five possibilities.

*Chapter V*

# Evaluation of the System by Tilliyard

The level of the direct and oblique poetry, subjects and medium and the criticism thereof, in the last two chapters, he has specifically manifested that the oblique-poetry is the only best. He has shown the importance of both direct and oblique poetry. He has stressed the importance of Oblique poetry in comparison with the direct poetry. In order that his ideology may be accepted, he has tried to evaluate the European poetry in each 'time' and he has tried to make an effective survey on this point ably - by criticising direct and Oblique poetry - both. This has gone to help prove that in every 'period', there has been a flow of direct poetry always. Hence in this chapter, we shall have a retrospection - a survey - on the direct poetry and in the end on the Oblique poetry by Tilliard's criticism thereon. We shall simultaneously value, while considering the value of both the types of poetries.

Before the 5th Century, Europe had not given thought on the system of indirect poetry, there was a traditional description of the subject, while undertaking the medium of oblique poetry. In the days of Homer, the presence of Gods in the literature proves this fact. There was a faith on Gods. By taking into consideration, different levels, subjects, and instruments and criticism and at last he propounds the theory that the oblique poetry is the best compared to all others. He is simultaneously all praise for direct poetry also but simultaneously he has again advocated that the importance in a comparative way is also a matter of pride for oblique poetry. In order to emphasise his views, he has taken into consideration european poetry in each time, and he has given comparative examples of both the type of poetries - viz. direct and oblique. It has been helpful to him because in each period, there has been a good easy flow of direct poetry only. Hence in this chapter we shall observe and have a birds-eye-view of the importance of direct poetry and its contemporary comparison with the obliqueness of the poetry by Tilliard. We shall evaluate on his method and fitness of his thoughts and criticism.

Before the 5th Century, when the Europe was not in a position to follow the system, there was a style where the description took prominence but still there was some importance of the medium of oblique poetry. In the time of Homer, the presence of the gods in the literature proves this theory. There was faith in gods and their presence in the poetry shows the confidence of the people in their minds about their existence. Homer has made the best use of this theory. But Uripidies etc. have made the use of the gods in their oblique style only. It is used as a medium to express themselves. In the 5th Century, when they resorted to self- expression, there was an increase in the formation by way of duping. Pseudo poetry came into being. There are examples of both type in the period of Elizabeth and there about - we have got examples of both the types. But in direct poetry, the evaluation is slowly tumbling down, due to helplessness and not due to psuedoism ! The poetry of those days is definitely exemplary. Goer can be said to be a representative of the direct poetry of that age. The translation in those days gave a lift to the poetical existence.

In the times of Eliszabethian period, all short of poetry came into picture. The decorative poetry also flowed like anything. There were poets as Denial, Dalton, Jhon Devy, and others, who made poetry as ordinary as drama for the public. The Don protested against this - the style of patronizing - and he proved by his own compositions, but Milton kept a balance in his composition - the reason was that he was alive of his duties towards the society. 18th Century was the climax of this period for direct poetry. In these days, we find Dryden, Tompson, and Pope as poets. In the poetry of Dryden, we find obliqueness in sufficient quantity, and yet he is an establisher of Direct poetry to a quite certain extent. He has given to the poetry a height and seriousness, which is quite different from Goyer. 'The Seasons' by Tompson is also a popular poetry in direct style. Pope too had written in this very style but there was absence of illumination and he wrote in his traditional style - he could not take the poetry ahead. Whereas in dryden, we get the best of his ability.

We now take a review of the 19th Century of Queen Victoria. This was the time when the direct poetry has had its fall and open-style with freedom of expression had been in vogue. It was not that at that time, there was no direct poetry, it was very much there, but at a low level - it was embellished with decorative, in explicit artificialness. In Browning we find the best society performance and again in Tennyson, we see the style of direct approach rising, but there was no co-operation between the two - Browning the Tennyson and hence they could not impress each other as it/they should. After that we come across - Cliff, Pentmore, Mrs. Browening who have adopted to this style and even to to-day this style has not gone out of fashion. Kipling, Mensfield, Miss selvile West are the poets of the 20th Century, but to-day we find that the poetry is dying out.

It is true that to-day the direct poetry is in the position of extinction - its position is even worse compared to the 19th Century. Not only that but also it announces that this type of poetry should come to an end. There are some reasons for that in the busy days of to-day's busy life, reader wants to have a poetry with there length and secondly they have no time to read these sort of direct poetry books. To-day's critic wishes to have the knowledge of the top-books. Under the circumstances, when he has no time, why should be waste this time towards or in reading the poetry of second standard. The third wishes to drive out the entire direct poetry composition from the field of poetry. They advocate that the such sayings should be narrative in prose and not in poetry.

But this is the one side of the picture. In support of direct poetry, many arguments could be advanced. First of all, Kipling, Mensfield, Miss Selvile West are the best examples who prove that the poetry is not dead. The tradition may have thinned down, but yet it continues. When one talks about the study of the top- books, when there would be only top-class books and there would not be existence of second class. But it is a fact that the second class compositions are there - they were very much there in the past, they are existence at present and they would remain present even in future.

In reality, in this context only the beauty of the top-class comes into being - the poetry shines out. For the sake of comparison, we can judge the first class, only when we have had the chance of tasting 2nd class in quite a good number. We cannot replace poetry in place of prose or vice versa. In the light of the best of the novel, we cannot compare it with a book of poetry. D.H. Lawrence is a quite well known prose writer, but we evaluate critically, both, his poetry-writing cannot stand in comparison with his prose compositions. Hence Best prose cannot and should not have a best poetry back-ground. The best prose/poetry could be the background of the best back-ground only which is full of relative qualities. Thus when the human beings would like to retain the existence of the poetry in its normal form, then the best poetry will have to be compared in the light of the direct poetry with the oblique poetry as well. We shall have to ameliorate the specialities of both.

After writing the whole book, the writer at the end raises a question. If we give a poetry a rank of a direct poetry or of a oblique poetry - whether we should criticise in one way or the other way. There are two views on this point. First is that for every individual the meaning of an oblique poetry is according to his own perception and understanding and whether we should consider it only as a fancy - a fanciful imagination. Secondly if it is accepted by the world openly, then will he lose his own individually. The writer is of the opinion that in the field of experience of the poet's writings, we shall have to give an appropriate place - a proper place as an individual and his merits. It is true that at times, he readers would come to a conclusion that the writer would not have dreamt of, but generally on an average reader, with a balanced mind, touches a particular level, and even though one has a difference of opinion agrees to the rightful meaning of the writer. And the excellence, exhaultment of the creation maintains its dignity individually.

Now a second question arises. Is there any benefit of such a criticism or a system of critical observation. In reply to this, we shall have to divide the readers in two categories. One is of the type which/who reaches to a deep level of understanding, to which the writer has already referred - they adjust in the environment of the writer. The second category is that, where one has to be trained to enjoy the benefits of the writer's views and feelings. Once the reader reads the original poetry and after that the criticism on that writing, he is in a position to enjoy the benefit of the writing. This is the benefit of the criticism- system.

After having gone through all this, when we compare the subject with the Indian Poetical literature, we shall have to have a retrospection. The book can be appreciated for brevity. Its style is pleasant, tasteful, simple and it is an important fact when we criticise this, we have to take into consideration one important fact that the writer has made an appreciable attempt to include western places of literature with interesting topics. We have before us 'Illiad', 'The Aneid', 'Paradise lost' and with this, we get into touch with Homer, Virgil and Milton's poetical richness; we read their own original pieces just for the sake of taste and variety. Black, Shailey Keats, Illiat, Yiets - all these great and big poets, and also Goldsmith, Mathew Arnold, Dryden, Pentmore and Meridieth - all these are dexterously incorporated woven in a neat and attractive fashion. Although much has been said about 'Millars's tale' and its oblique interpretation, and it is not necessary that every one should agree to/with this, but still however we shall have to observe openly that 'The Echoing Green', 'The Sick Rose' and 'Illiad' - in the analysis/criticism of all these the writer has shown his own individuality and proved his merits unquestionably. The writer is quite well-read, and yet he has his own limitations and atmosphere and as such angle-difference is bound to be there. But still his efforts must be appreciated to reach the suggestions of the poetical construction of Indian Poetical literature. Our hats are off to him - undoubtedly - without an iota of exaggeration.

*Chapter VI*

# Tilliard's Observation of Indian Poetry

The Book 'Poetry' - Direct and Oblique was published by Dr. E.M.W. Tilliard, Litt. D. Uni. Lecturer in English and Fellow of Jesus College, Cambridge, in the year 1934 - published by 'Chatt & Windus', London.

Although it appears to be small, still it has achieved its own name and fame due to its establishment, clear observation and criticism and appropriate relevant examples from Indian/English Literature, as the case may be. He has made it a herculean effort in writing this book. It come into the category of an authoritative publication. The writer is very conscious about his writings and in his efforts, he has put arguments and questions and counter questions on both the sides - right from the asking to its appropriate reply. His thoughtfulness goes deep into the depth of the poetry and tries to reveal the secret of the thought of the writer/composer. There are observations on the Greek Literature in the beginning and leaving that he has mainly banked upon the european literature only. It reveals the mental state of the freedom of thought of those days and it has taken quite some efforts to make the picture clear describing the difficulties of the days of yore. In talks less about reality. It has a philosophical approach only.

It will not be an exaggeration when we say that the angle towards reality was not there. Tilliard in the 20th century, with the help of this book he has tried to take a judgement according to his own angle. But in reality, the Indian Poetical approach is always towards factual reality. It is due to this that even before 1000 years we have books like 'Dhwanyalok' and 'Vakṛokti Jivitam'. It involves a system of criticism in the Indian poetic field. Towards this end, the westerners have now only diverted their attention. In the past chapters we have tried to give a pro-forma of the principle of Obliqueness by Tillyard. Now, in this chapter we shall try to have a comparative study of Indian and Western poetic principles, as far as it relates to both the fields.

**Classification of the Poetry**

According to Indian poetical history, in the beginning, Acharya Dandi tried to establish the principles of separation compartment in a systematic orderly manner by dividing the compositions in the two sectors - natural expression and second oblique expression. It is not that this principle was not known before Dandi. In the writings of Bhamah, we can find the possibilities of this, but even then in Dandi only we get the right evaluation/direction. Kuntak has accepted this division and he too has accepted the importance of direct method.

And having taken into consideration this division, the importance of direct method, he as a matter of competition, the position of obliqueness in the poetry, he composed the book called 'Vakrokti Jivitam' meaning Oblique assessment. This is a wonderful book in its originality and one should study this to comprehend Indian poetry. The writer Bhoj divides the poetry into three section : (i) Direct - natural sayings - (ii) Oblique sayings (iii) 'Rasa' (Character) saying (A saying which has one of the nine characteristics of taste of the poetry). He advocates that Natural sayings is based on quality, obliqueness saying is based on decoration, and character-sayings is based on the 'taste' - the inner taste in contains. It is an accepted fact that this division has in principle accepted by the poets, in one-way or be other. those who are advocates of 'suggestion' - principle, or in other words 'sound Principles' are not congruent to this advocacy - they are separate in their thinking against this division, but still it cannot be said that it can be said to be devoid of this principle of 'oblique-poetry' in toto.

Tillyard has given the name of his book - the title of the book as 'Poetry - Direct and Oblique' and with the help of these two rods, he has tried to divide the poetry in these two divisions - and it manifests that the poetry is divided into two clear sections a direct poetry and another oblique poetry. Tillyards' this usage, without doubt, rests this demarcation on the Indian Poetical version of 'slant-saying' (Vakrra-slant-Uktt-Saying). On this very basis of this, we come to two divisions such as 'Direct-expression' and 'Oblique - expression. When we read the entire book, we can come to the conclusion (which matter is very clear in the first chapter only) that the use of the word 'Oblique' is not in the 'oblique' sense, but in the sense of 'Irony' only. According to him, if a poetry touches only the professed subject and stresses effectively on the main subject only, it is an expression/narration by way of 'direct' method only. But when the meaning, in reality, touches to a hidden meaning or it side tracks the meaning from the original meaning. It cannot be said to be a 'direct' method, but only 'Vakra (Oblique/slanting) K-avya' only. This is not directly related to the direct meaning. It flows from all the frame of the poetry. Anandvardhan acharya in his book Dhwanyalok Shloka 1/13, manifests the same principle. They talk about the 'sound' - a suggestion' of the poetry and how ?

The Shloka quoted above directs that - when meaning de-littles the original meanings and directs the reader to refer to another meaning, other than the one quoted in the words, the literate people call it 'Sound' or 'suggestion' which manifests, emphasises its beauty.

Here we again quote Shloka No. 1/14 from Dhwanyalok, which means - That what is something else, and the beauty of the ladies' face, eyes, ears, and separate from the beauty, the great writers have said quite different in their sa-yings.

Whatever Tillyard has told is not the equivalent of Kutank's expression. In Direct Poetry, he has incorporated the following six divisions :

1. Reinforced Statement.
2. Philosophical
3. The statement supported by Onomato-poeia
4. The statement supported by Rhyme/Rythm.
5. Embroidered Statement.
6. Disguised

If oblique was the word of Kuntak's idea, in side the direct poetry only first two divisions would have been incorporated. The remaining four comes into category of Obliqueness. In the entire book, the attention of the writer is mainly based on the oblique meaning only. He has commented upon accessories, but he has not stressed the point anywhere, where it is not more than necessary. Whereas the Kuntak's entire criticism is based on observation and planning. Tillyard has paid attention to the great poems of Western culture and it has taken more time than anything else. Whereas Kuntak's oblique interpretation is based on the planned programme by giving its full descriptions. In reality, Tillyard has wrongly selected the word 'oblique' in the place of 'indirect' which would have been more appropriate. Or to be more effective, the word 'suggestive' should have been better. Meaning to say the criticism of Tillyard should have been on the principles of 'Dhwani' - 'Sound' and not on the basis of 'Obliqueness'. But then we cannot ignore the fact that his statement is not away from obliqueness.

As far as there is question of divisions, we can serially divide them into two categories - 'Direct' and 'Oblique'. We can call them 'direct delivery - a direct statement and/or 'suggestive or indirect - oblique statement, according to context and composition Anandvardhan acharya classifies both as concealed irony and the sounding-sentiment. In the ironical statement, the main meaning is set aside and Tillyard does not agree with this statement; He is of the opinion that there cannot be a poem with direct meaning only; there is bound to be somewhere 'oblique' meaning concealed somewhere which makes the poetry a poetry. There is some slant/some irony some ambiguity somewhere. Whereas in every poetry there is some suggestive thought, which creates the poetry interesting. Anandvardhan has also created a third division also, which relates to 'picturesque presentation', but Tillyard does not touch to this topic at all. Mammtacharya has classified this picturesque poetry as 'third rate', because it has no 'sound/or suggestion therein. However Tillyard refers to 'Disguised Statement' in his book. Because in the disguised statement, there is no ornamentation, nor towards the main meaning nor does strengthen the main interpretation and hence this sort of picturesque poetry is void and devoid of any meaning.

The two divisions of the poetry, namely, direct and oblique has been divided by Tillyard in six divisions and again into two subsections. But he has not been in a position to explain the divisions of the oblique poetry. He has taken into consideration only the side-issues and the principle subject. The three divisions made by him, viz. ornamental-sounding, subject- touching, interest-sentimental-touch, which are simultaneously interpreted as sentimental, main thoughts, and original tendencies. But in reality he has failed in assessment to a certain extent. The great expectations and its formation have been treated by him in the form of a criticism and in assembling he loses control over the subject matter and in contacting original native qualities, the qualities such as fear, compassion and pleasure

- these are not properly handled as it should have been. It has not touched the Indian poetic sentiments at all. Whereas in reality, there is some balance between decoration, and sentiments and Tillyard has failed to take into consideration that even the decorative treatment can be effectively sounded. If it is properly handled, because in western literature, there is no scope for ornamentalisation, as is done in Indian and hence the western world is not aware of this delicacy. Moreover Tillyard is not prepared to accept the system of reaching to the main meaning directly or indirectly. He tries to establish that he is the founder of this system and then he himself puts up question as to whether this system as beneficial at all ? And then he himself answers that his system teaches the readers about that what he wishes to convey. In Reality, Anandvardhan, 1000 years back, he had established/emphasised this system, & proved that how the theme touches the sentiment of the writer and the reader both. There is no doubt about this. The writer Anandvardhan has identified the main sentiment of the poetry as an ironical expression and he has proved its utility in the main stream, and he has manifested that there is no other system other than this one to touch the delicate meaning of the poetic composition.

## THE SPHERE OF OBLIQUE POETRY

### 1. Sensitiveness

Tillyard has divided obliqueness into three divisions. The first is sensitiveness. The meaning there of is the composition of words, dexterity of colourful description, it creates an impression on our sense and creates a silent sensation which leads to touchiness, and to arouse the imagination that it would leads to touchiness, and to arouse the imagination that it would carry us to a land of fantasy. Our mind would fly far and wide. The quietness of senses is the main achievement of this - these qualify their qualities and sentimental touch is the direct result thereof. Onomatopoeia gives strength to the subject of the poetry, but sentimental sensitiveness takes us away from the subject and leads us to the land of different experiences. This sensitiveness is not a dry subject of the observation of the rules and regulations of the composition of the poetry, but it is created out of the delicate touch which is piercing powerfuly and appeals to the inner conscience. We do not get much response to this in occidental literature, but western literature is full of all these. Our criticism is not in a position to open the gates of criticism. But in Sanskrit literature, you will not find this in absence. There is some effect of this on Hindi literature and it is interesting to observe that it is plentily available in the impressive poetry and principle poetry. New Poetry which has a backing of progressive group has tried to oppose this by way of principle, but impressionists (Chhayavadi) have made the use of this in many ways, Sometimes it has come before us in a very powerful form. For example, we can take Dinkar's Urvashi - Pages 44 and 70 - which are both the examples of the experience of Pururava in the beginning of his search. In first it takes the reader to the electric touch of Urvashi and Pururava, right away from the existing world. In reality the touch is so decisive that it touches the delicate core of the heart. In second the reader's mental vista is widened and in the absence of both - Urvashi and Pururava, it deluges in a super natural feelings, which beggars description. This sensitiveness touches the 'Ironical' approach of Urvashi with our inner soul. The reader feels this touchy because the writer has touched to 'ironical' set up - in the words of Tillyard 'Oblique' or 'Urvashi'. He writes:

"There is woman hidden in a woman which is body-less and beyond all the physical senses. Man comes in contact with this when the mental waves throw the man into the feelings of ocean and it reaches to a level which is beyond the bodily experience and it reaches to a state of 'sumum bonum', where it rests in peace. 'in the same way, in the same category, on the same wave-length, there is man hidden in a man, which does not rest on the body surface; in the frenzy to touch the senses of the body of a woman, he reaches beyond a level, which cannot be caught in words."

"The couple, which is tied in an indescribable feeling wants to reach that world which is full of light and air."

Tilliyard has quoted in his book excerpts from Tennisan and Pope but yet and still our occidental environmental experiment and experience is much more deeper and effective that the western ones. Sensitiveness of sentiment is not the only quality. Whatever Tillyard has quoted about Great Commonplace, about oblique poetry, he has given ample justice to his efforts in this direction - there is no doubt about it.

**2. The Great Commonplace**

Tillyard has placed these great commonplace to such an high exhaulted position that it can be compared with the 'Angiras's imagination of a grand and great existence. This is sounded as a suggestive of 'unlisted' 'Irony'. It is description has been considered as a 'Defect'. The sound which is comes out of 'Angiras', gives such a sound that to reach the climax, the inner qualities such as 'goodness', 'decoration', the plot - all these are helpful to a great extent. These are the beauties of the "great Commonplace". In a full poetry, there are mainly two forms; (1) In our suggestive attempt, it draws towards the human touch of a human being, but still there is a material difference in the approach. Angiras is the exhibition of a human tendency where as 'Great commonplaces' touch to the thoughtful intelligence. Angiras touches the love aspect and it explauds and takes one to the result thereof - to the maturity - but the great commonplace is the result of the penance of great thoughts. Because it deals with the thoughtfulness great commonplace may exceed in number, but the literature has selected Angiras for its nine 'Rasas' such as 'Rati', Shok' 'Utsah' and 'Nirved'. In reality angiras is the expression of personal experience in person. these four sentiments have been considered in the life, the principle effective elements. It digests the feelings of human life in a balanced away. Lastly in must be borned in mind that the common place, to be of the highest effect, must be powerfully and consistently dominant - page 49.

We refer to Pream's Echaias episode, when the dead body of the Hector is demanded - this is a graphic description of the 'tragedy' climax. The death of the Echailis' son, has become the effective impact on the mind of Pream and the 'Pain' touches his heart too. Thus in fine, we can conclude that the great commonplace is the description of the intelligent description of a great creation, and Angiras becomes its mouthpiece. In the final conclusion, both the definitions lead us to a great experience. It exhibits the great height. I will confirm this by giving an example from our 'Ramcharit Manas'.

If we leave aside the circumstantial atmosphere, there is comparative similarity between the 'Illiad' and the story of 'Ramcharit Manas Katha' - one side there is kidnaping of Hellen - other side there is that of 'Sita'. Hellen has gone out of her own will whereas Sita has been kidnaped. The route cause of the War/Battle is the carrying away of a woman against social custom - against all principles of morality and ethics. The description of both the Wars is principally based on this very principle of immorality quoted above.

In both the gods have participated. If see with a balanced mind, the principle 'Rasa' - Interest - is 'War Spirit'. Here we do not believe in Tulsi, but we resort to Rama only. If we take resort to Tulsi, there would be a different oblique meaning and hence in fine, we take resort to the principle characters of both the stories and not the writers. But then the question arises whether and when Tillyard takes the resort to the death of Hector and he refers to this great expectation, is it the only resort to the main book ? The answer then is in the negative. This is the description of one of the incidents of the Tilliyard and if take resort to oblique meaning, there is no other factor than the national pride. Tillyard has taken this very point into consideration and he has resorted to the great expectation. This is not the only expectation hidden from beginning to end in the 'Illiad'. We can create many more expectations on different occasions in 'Illiad'. In a different mood we can say that it is full of thoughtful thoughts. If we take on a delicate base, we can show even a small incident as its base. After having beheaded the head of Meghnad by the arrow of Lakshmana and his (Meghnad's) head to make reach the inner chamber of 'Sulochana' and the corpse remains in the possession of the army of 'Rama'. There is quite a similar similarity like Sulochana going for the body of the Meghnad to the army of Rama; this incident identically depicted in 'Illiyad' when the dead body of the Hector is asked for by his father to the assasinator. At the place of 'Pream', there is a woman, and at the place of son, there is body of husband. It is to be observed critically that there is no difference in the principle.

The difference is there when in the place of Rama, there is placement of Echailis, considering the Rama as God. It is true that the incident does not create that impact as in Illiad, but when we take into consideration the subject of 'compassion' or to be precise 'Tragedy' Illiad gets more marks in this direction. Tillyard has expressed this as the exhibition of passions - In his words - (It could supply the student of passions with the most exciting material). To conclude, I would say that the interest (Rasa) when absent, the great expectations becomes baseless and it could succeed only when it is suggestive and explicit both at once.

It is an accepted version that 'Ramcharit Manas' by 'Tulsi' is a complete thing as such, with the principle 'Rasa' is 'Vira Rasa'. But then the question arises whether there is any great expectations sounded by Tillyard or 'Ramcharit manas' is the expression of various 'Rasas' combined together. The answer is very clear. Illiad with all its expectations for human values - on account of its basic principles it suggests towards basic instinct of human beings. The principle of 'One man's wife' - consideration of a 'Sati' - because the principle of Indian ideology is absent in western culture in toto. It would be out of place to expect Indian Ideology in Western depict or in western thoughts. Illiyad is a Greek Poetry, whereas 'Ramacharitmanas' is a version of - exhibition of - advocate of basic Indian culture. 'Ramacharit Manas' does not speak at any place about 'Sati culture'.

But we can definitely say that the writer's angle is quite high and in nature extraordinary. If we refer to the oblique interpretations of 'Manas', we may conclude that - Manas completely rejects any individual identity - and the basis of this evasion is the culture of 'Bhakti' - devotion - complete devotion at all costs. If you take into consideration the spirit of Lisides with the spirit of 'Manas' it leads towards the great expectations and in a very serious measurement and both are compared at a right level. It is possible that the oblique angel of 'Ramayan' - all the three principles of the knowledge of three instincts - Satva, Raja and Tamasa, Knowledge and action and its balance may tackle as imbalance in comparison of the two and the 'Lokayatan' may exceed the great expectation - the spirit of the people - but yet 'Manas' is such a great poetry that it remains balanced in all its aspects and it is in no way less than the comparison of 'Illiyad' The principle here is not to analyse each one with the other, and to brand one as greater than the other, far from it; we would like to visualise that although the principles, circumstances, atmosphere, culture may be different in both, but even then we find a subtle similarity between the two, as if one is complement to the other and vice versa; it cannot be called 'Oblique poetry' because of the style, but thought in both is worth giving attention to - one cannot ignore the great depth with which each one is full - although separate separately in themselves, and yet it pleads a notion of nationality.

**Human tendencies**

Because Tillyard is a westerner, he has not the slightest idea about 'Rasa' - Sentiment in a poetry written in India (Especially in Original Sanskrit language). He has had not the slightest experience about its depth, delicacy and duo-meaningful compositions of occidental atmosphere. That does not mean that he is not an appreciator of the Poetry - he is very much what he is: Any critic cannot afford to ignore its (poetry's) substance-conveyance nor accept its presence invariably. Tillyard has his own belief. He believes that the obliqueness of the poetry is a part and parcel of of the compositor's composition and it can not be separated like soul from the body. He has termed 'Human tendencies' under the impact of 'fear', 'Pleasure' and 'misery'. Whereas in Indian Poetical tradition has described 9 tendencies attached to a composition; there is nothing beyond that. In a poetry, there is a fixed tendency (Sthayi Bhava), which is the soul of the composition; Possibly Tillyard has had no occidental back-ground and as such as has interpreted that the oblique/slang/Slant saying only in an ironical way is the soul of the poetry. In Indian tradition, we come across, Bhav-Shabalta, Bhav-Shanti and many other tendencies, which are subtlely attached to main theme. Tillyard has put before us examples of Turns, Pelinras and he has tried to explain to us how the meaning can be taken a side/astray - which is quite impossible otherwise. We can say that much only that he has not been able to successfully delineate between Indian 'Bhava' and 'Rasa' - Sentiment and tendency. According to Indian poetry, even without using the words of 'Pain' and 'Pleasure', the criticism will lead one to a field of imaginary touch. Whether 'Pathos' is a matter of 'Happiness' or otherwise - this is the main question with the Indian poetry. Dr. Nagendra has tried to establish the 'Pleasure- feeling' converted in 'Pathos' and it is a wave of human tendency, which seeks the roots of the human nature. The rest also leads a matter of satisfaction. This is the definition of Dr. Nagendra. Of course, there is no similarity between Dr. Nagendra and Tillyard, but yet the latter is inclined towards the usefulness of the poetry. He (the latter) does agree with the former at times, and that is the reason why Tillyard also keeps faith on life very deeply and he says that:

"For those who felt the burden of self consciousness too heavy thoughts of escape were the inevitable consequence while those who accepted the burden cannot have lacked some misgivings at 1st. In all poetry where the problem enters there must needs be some nostalgia present. It is where the melancholy is isolated from the joy which initially engendered it that there is a vicious nostalgia. The true joy melancholy means full acceptance of the situation and the courage not to go back on the primal human commitment."

The above quotation proves that his tender heart is ready enough to touch the core of the subject, but the boundaries thereof make him unable to cross the limit.

## INSTRUMENTS FOR OBLIQUENESS

**1. The Tune**

We have seen in the past that Tillyard has divided his work on this subject in two main divisions:

The tune, with the help of Onomatopoeia makes the poetry quite strong. This helps a lot in the formation, construction, composition of a poetry. 2. And when this very tune makes a change and with the help of any other instrument, it takes away from the main theme of the subject But in doing so, it changes the meaning of the expression altogether; This sort of tune is termed Oblique-tune, and whatever meanings he has discussed is the sensitiveness and human tendencies. For touchy subject, he has selected Poet's petrity style and he has quoted his examples and for human tendencies, he has selected the 'Aneid' and the plot of Paineneres; and also Hymn of Pan by Shailey.

In Indian Poetic science, the main two elements which are mainly discussed here and they are rhyme and rhythm. There are many examples in Sanskrit and Hindi Languages in support of the above-mentioned theories, which make the subject matter very strong and effective. On account of onomatopeia, it touches the main subject effectively but simultaneously it is easy to speak, spell and pronounce. The poetry in Sanskrit and Hindi are full of these examples. There are different styles/systems by which the same spoken words and their tunes create a marvellous impressions on the minds of readers and hearers both; the repetition makes the rhyme and rhythm show majestically.

It is very interesting to observe the system, the method, the trial on which these are based; The same letter is repeated often and often, but every time, it makes a different meaning - direct and oblique - and thus creating a juglary of words and creating an atmosphere of spell-bound phenomena. This you will be able to find only in Indian theme, Indian poeticism, Indian culture. It cannot be ignored if is mentioned that there has been incidents of the disadvantage of this situation; but that does not mean that the original beauty is not there. With the rhyme, if we refer to the meter, it controls the poetic composition and it gives them the beauty of a beautiful status as far as Indian poetical History is concerned. By and with the help of Meter, they have carved out in history their names in golden letters. Of course, various experiments were in process and it could not be out of place, if we term it as a Museum and we have a book on meters by a writer named 'Museum of Meters' (Ram Chandrika) This is has been proved that the Meter and the subject matter are very knitly/closely related/attached. One cannot to without the other. In the composition style of 'sur' and 'Mira', one would not expect 'Bravery' in their compositions nor do we expect 'Shrungar' and allied subjects in the folk-lore couplets. Thus one has to be wary about the choice - if one expects magic at every place, it is not possible - it is just impossible. The relation of Meter and rhyme touches the subject aptly.

The Onomatopoeia, the Rhythm, Pause and Rhyme, all these go for the formation of a beautiful poetry only; it is through this only that the subject matter is depicted. The main question is that whether where is any provision in Indian Poetry, whereby, with the help of Onomatopeia, rhyme and Rhythm only one can approach the suggestive meaning of the main theme. The Book 'Vakrokti Jivitam' discusses about the details about oblique poetry but regarding rhyme and meter the book is silent. There is some mention about alliteration and rhyme somewhere but that is the only discussion about the main theme of the poetry. Tillyard too has confirmed that with the help of rhyme only we can touch the main theme. In the Book 'Dhwanyalok' also there is no mention about rhyme or meter and the derivation of the meaning through the instrumentality of these medium. In the Books dealing with the meters, there is only mention about that particular subject only and they do not guide us about the approach to the real meaning of the theme depicted. In the Books of Meters (Chhand Shashtra Books), they discuss about the different meters and their specialities by giving suitable examples on the subject. They have not elaborated on the topic of the Theme or approach to the subject, and with the medium of 'Obliqueness' we cannot expect these books to elucidate further in th~ i atter. It is possible to investigate these through the medium of 'Epic' or 'Lyric', as to where the that subject about meter stands. In the Bigger poetical compositions there are descriptions of various places; they differ according to place and environment and they - the composers - resort to different meters, as they are available for description.

The arrangement of change in meter, according to music, it can be said that this is for the sake of oblique meaning to which to poet refers to. The poet may wish to convey that (1) in the next chapter, I shall resort to this particular meter (2) or in the next chapter I would like to describe that subject matter which is more or less related to this particular meter. Thus this would enhance the delicacy of the poetry. The second meaning of the poetry could be taken out only when the poet is prepared for that - in that case, he can arrange for separate meters, when he has decided to do so. But according to the rules of the literature, this sort of change in the meter would be more or less traditional and there would lesser scope for the oblique interpretation.

So far as the question of the usage of rhyme for the sake of Oblique utility, we can come across many examples in books like "Geet Govinda" or 'Megh-doot', where there are many examples of sensitiveness or human tendencies. But to put rhyme in live activeness, one has to be very active in the usage and formation thereof. There are modern poetries with this particular touch. As far as sensitiveness is concerned, we can refer to the writer 'Dharmvir. Bharati', or 'Anupriya' or 'Dinkar', which are very rich in all the respect. It will not be possible for us to quote Hindi couplets of Urvashi by Dinkar, an account of printing difficulties - we however mention in English wording, the Hindi poetry, reading -

*'Kya Vishavas kare Koi, Kalpanamayi is Dhi Ka,*
*Amit bar deti Hai Chhalana Bhej Tirth-pathinkon, Ko,*
*Us Mandir ki Aur Kahin jiska astitva nahin hai.'*

The rhyme - the tune of these lines gives us that wide vista, which takes us to a land far away from beyond and leaves us in that state of sentiment that there is no scope for oblique interpretation.

But it creates a sensation of intelligence, which creates a situation which beggars description. It is true that after reading these lines, we reach to that mental situation where the justification is to be given to the impression of the lines. But here the main obliqueness is that of the rhyme only; there is one another quotation from very 'Urvashi' -

> *'O Shunya pavan main muze dekh chumban arpit karne valo....... Adharon main apane adharon ki madira uden yugon ki sanchit tapan mitaungi.'*
>
> *(Urvashi Pages 99-100).*

There is up and down in the rhyme. The subject of the poetry describe the man's psychological and woman's natural instincts and it takes to a depth of inner mind but the rhyme takes us to a second side of the woman's which is the oblique meaning of the poetry - this is an indication and reality both. The first two lines makes us travel in a direction of a long journey step by step exactly in the same manner as a wave length of the ocean takes to a distance of the wave length and touches the bank of the sea. after that there are three small lines, wherein compared to first and third, the second one is quite elaborate. The mind gets varegated with the expansion/contraction and the long line, and the first few words stops for a moment and the reader is stunned in the same position. 'Sarita Samudra Giri Van more Avadhan nahin' - here the alliteration and repetition of certain letters takes the reader to a long journey and stops on the words 'Vishvapriya' and then the reader proceeds further and goes through further four lines. The entire poetry is full of word-selection, stress on the letters, alliteration, usage of novels, pause and stop - it is so symbolitically complete in all respects that it gives easy delivery and it swings the mind rhythmatically in the process of expansion and concentration and thus creates that mental satisfaction that the reader would not like to get out of the impact - the cadence - for some time to come.

> *'Kshna Kshna pragate dure, chhipe, fir fir jo chumban lekar....*
> *Purush bade sukh se rahata hei, us pramada ke vash main.*
>
> *(Page 35- 36).*

According to my opinion, this poetical piece tries to impress the reader with the help of rhyme obliqueness - The poet wishes to convey about a woman who mesmerises the man with the art of impression, but this he has done not only through the words, but through the medium of rhyme also. Urvashi is the representative of the women kind, but she is not that of the type of 'Aushinari' - She is a woman and not anything else. This obliqueness has its own meaning. The rhyme itself strengthens the subject but it is not onomatopoiatic. This rhyme exhibits the woman by its obliqueness, which is altogether a different subject. The subject is also strengthened. It is possible that all the readers may not agree with my expression, my thoughts, my interpretation; but it is my experience, my feelings, my impression. Everyone - including the critics - may not accept my version, but as it is, so it is, as is depicted, as is written, it is an out-birst of one's own feelings and it is quite true that all the feelings and interpretation may not be alike.

**The Symbol System**

As has been told in the past, Tillyard has used 'Symbol' in a limited way and in this connection he has told us about three points:

1. The symbol is associated with the writer to depict some symbolical decision associated with the symbol.
2. Even if you remove the symbol from the subject matter, it has its own independent existence and in a separate form, it discloses some specific oblique interpretations.
3. Although the use of symbol in a poetry, distracts the mind of the reader and it establishes from the main topic and concentrates on the topic only and but that does not mean that it reduces the meaning of the poetry. Out of the subject matter of the symbolical poetry, whatever irony it produces, the reader takes out many meanings out of that.

In our Indian Life, right from time of Vedas, we have symbols in the fields of Religions, Philosophical, Pauranik, and Social fields. An emblem of a Pot, Coconut, Flame, Light, fire-fly, Swan Swastik - there are thousand and one symbols/emblems, but in Sanskrit literature, we do not come across the definition which Tillyard wishes to convey in his writings. He refers to Kuntak's Vakrokti - Jivitam'. He refers to deliberate obliqueness, the science of Sound/suggestion comparative basis of indications and displacement of the original meaning, and in the criticism he refers to the symbols and emblems. But all these come in the fore-front only to strengthen the main subject; not in the form of any in-direct meaning. It will be in-correct to arrive at the usage of 'Lakshan-Lakshana' is based on the fact that it is there to strengthen the original meaning. In reality the eritic poets have tried to impress themselves by using this many fold symbolic introduction in their poems. But still this does not come in the form of symbolic system. I will corroborate my statement by quoting the famous couplet of Bihari-

*'Lakh Gurujan Vich Sis sau Kamal Chhuayo Syam,*
*Hari Sanmukh Kari AArsi, Hiye lagaye Ham."*

Meaning - Radha was sitting amongst the seniors; Krishna saw her; He applied the lotus flower to his head and in reply to that action, Radha showed the mirror towards the Sun and it (the mirror) was applied by Radha to her heart.

Now the *real* meaning - we shall have to analyse the meaning of each word to come to arrive at the real meaning expressed in these lines. 'Lotus' is the symbol of a 'feet' and the word 'Hari' is the synonym of 'Sun' and 'Krishna' and now the indirect meaning is like this-

Krishna applies the lotus to his head, meaning He bows to the lotus feet of Radha and in reply Radha took the impression of Sun in her mirror meaning the impression of Lord Krishna in the mirror and applied the mirror to her heart. (this means that the impression Lord Krishna is always in the heart of Radha).

**Hence the Ironical/Oblique meaning:**

According to Indian Custom and sociology, generally Man does not touch the feet of a woman, but we shall have to translate this unusual exchange terminology in a different aspect - with a different angle; meaning to say Lord Krishna requested Lady Radha to meet near the Lotus grove and the lady, having taken into consideration the public observation, she suggested that they should meet at the time of sun-set between two hills.

Now, it is very interesting to observe that all the three interpretations, translations, meanings have a varied subject, as to how the translator translates, interprets according to his own convenience and understanding. This is the beauty, subtlety, depth of the Sanskrit Poetic Literature. Unless one guides, what it is, one is at a cross road of ignorance and it may be that the reader may just skip over the writing without taking the trouble to go into the depth of the creation.

Here in this poetry the Lotus cannot be said to have been used as a symbol - it has been used as an object/subject of comparison. This couplet definitely comes into the purview of Tillyard, but this oblique meaning is due to the subject matter and due to symbolism. If you remove Lotus from the couplet, it does not interpret any other significant meaning. We also refer here to the 'Sick rose',where the 'rose' signifies the delicate bed as oblique meaning, but here in Lotus-bed one cannot imagine the meaning of sleep, because lotus carries the meaning of chastity.

In hindi literature, there is abundance of 'Nath' 'Siddha'and 'Sant'poets, who have used/manipulated symbols of 'Yoga' in the form of comparison only. The meaning there to are also deep- routed. The followers of this cult do not interpret any other meaning. In reality the use of symbols came into use from'Chhaya- vad' age; so far as Tillyard has put its use as an instrument of obliqueness. In the book 'Kavyalochan' the criticism on symbolic-usage, is due to English independent movement. In Indian poetry, in 'Dhwanyalok', there is comment on symbolism and in this context he has quoted the following shloka from Geeta:

> *"Ya Nisha Sarvabhutanam.......*
> *Sa Nisha pashyato Mune:"*

Lord God Krishna preaches Arjun in Geeta that the night creates one sort of illusion in the minds of ignorant who do not value knowledge as one should. Being ignorant, being away from knowledge, one sleeps in despair - at that very time, those who are not ignorant, or those have knowledge, and those who know themselves, these 'Yogi' people keep wide awake. They always make efforts to get knowledge and shun ignorance - philosophically - and that is how the ignorent resort to physical sleep, whereas those who are awake through the instrumentality of knowledge, keep awake - and thus those who know, keep away from 'passion'. And hence one should try to get real 'knowledge' in the best possible way. The writer of 'Dhwanyalok' has correctly criticised further on this point elaborately to make one understand the correct meaning of the correct interpretation:

He says that here 'Night' and 'Awakening' are the words do not relate to worldly interpretations, but they drive at 'Knowledge' and ignorance' - efforts to get real knowledge and efforts to get rid of 'ignorance' - these are the basic philosophical interpretation of this beautiful Shloka. One should keep faith in spiritual knowledge and not keep attached to involved into worldly base ideology leading to the passion and subsequent destruction of one's self.

In this shloka 'Night' and 'awakening' are in the form of real symbols - which through light on 'Ignorance' and 'Knowledge'. The oblique meaning of the very shloka would also lead one to the same meaning. It leads us to the sins which may be committed at night time, and to protect one from such indecent commitment, one has to resort to real correct knowledge. This very fact is true about 'Awakening' - it is not physical awakening, but awakening of the inner soul by way of real knowledge to be obtained from the 'shashtras' or through the medium of right 'Guru'. There is a long tradition of western symbolic interpretation and hence Tillyard has ignored the saying of 'Dhwanikar' and given his own independent views as has been said herein heretofore. But it can be said in fine that 'Dhwanikar' was fully familiar with the interpretation of 'symbolism's, which has been brought by Tillyard during the period of 20th century.

### 3. Unconnected Literary reference

Sometimes there are reference about unconnected literary reference, but Indian Literature have never accepted them towards the increasing beauty of the literature - nor they have commented upon them. But in reality, in our day to day life, this experiment has been so involved that it has become an ordinary routine matter in our literature. All critical reference books are full of such comparative criticisms. In to-day's time, such reference are openly resorted to. We may refer to Dr. Nagendra's Book 'Ras Sidhant's 'Nivedan' - last line - 'It is very difficult to delineate the authoritative back ground but when a man gets used to it, the pain becomes pleasure.

Here the writer has referred to 'Saket' by Maithilisharan Gupta, and by doing so, he has made his own statement more subtle, sweet and strengthful - it indeed difficult to mention that 'Here the labour is also pleasurable' The writer's observance is that the composition of the poetry is definitely difficult, but to create an authoritative observation is also and all the more difficult to attain it. To take interest in such work is quite laborious then to take pleasure in it.

To-day's poet is well-read; he has studied all the compositions from India ànd abroad. And due to this in his sayings, there are at times references to foreign literature also. For reference, please refer to Shree Gupta's one incident. When Ram Hears about the attack on 'Lakshmana' by means of 'Lakshmana-Shakti', he gets excited. And when Ram faces Kumbhakarana, he claims that 'brother for brother' and Rama kills Kumbhakarana. But when he sees Ravana before him, his excitement calms down at once. He feels the feeling of Ravana of being 'Brother-less' and in his deep within, he too feels the loss of his own brother; and he quotes:

> *'Oh Brother, come, we forget enmity, we both are miserable friends, Come let us embrace and makes our eyes pure.*
>
> *But Alas, but before he can express himself and his feelings, the Ravana fainted, and Rama too fainted expressing himself that - Ravanas in a better sensitive person - sincere person - that Rama"*

Here comes an indirect reference - the comparison of Rama and Ravana's 'Brother-loss' with the similarity of circumstances of 'Iliad' This refers to the scene of Son-Loss suffering of Prime and the dialogue between Echàilis gives a comparable similarity between the two tragic situation - one is about the loss of brother - the second is about the loss of a son. One is Occidental and the other is oriental, but the pangs of pain - one felt by brother, the other felt by father both baggers description. That great expectations between the two ideas is that the elements which try to divide the two feelings are less then the elements which try to join the two elements together. A direct reference is between the 'Needle' and a 'Pair of Scissors'. The first tries to join two together - the other separates the two. This is very interesting to observe about the subtle human tendencies with each person, with which each is over-run, over-whelmed. The good always conquers evil - this is the main interpretation.

Such reference is also available in 'Lokayatan' in 'Kalakar' Chapter Vignan - Here the poet takes his character poet to Greece, Rome, Egypt, France and Russia and also to Eastern Countries. This incident clearly indicates towards 'Shailey's 'Elster', where there is a reference of itinerary-minded youth, who undertakes the travels of the world. In this very way, 'Kamayani' on page 186 refers to the last seen in the same way. Although we can observe that in to-day's New Poetry, we find reference referred more to 'Pauranik Period's, but then, it is not void of the present day incidents and events too, when needed so.

**4. Poetical Obliqueness/Plot-obliqueness**

About this, Tillyard has divided 3 sections as under:

1. Excited passionate human excitement/tendencies, which are united and centrally established and shows poet's greatness.
2. It exposes the Great expectations.
3. He plans skillfully the plot narration and events. Kuntak in his book 'Vakrokti Jivitam' has divided this obliqueness in nine divisions:

1. Being of a state of sentimental situation.
2. Research of the presence.
3. Imagination about that which is absent.
4. The relation of the chapters with the Main plot.
5. Pleasure of a special chapter.
6. Description of Water-Resort or other such incidents and its tasteful description.
7. In order to arrive at the main event, resorting to sub-events.
8. In-drama in main drama
9. The relation of each chapter with the preceding one.

He has enumerated six divisions of main-obliqueness as under:

1. Change in the main-theme 'Rasa'. 2. The end of the story by means of the Main Character's sublimation which makes him reach pinnacle of glory. 3. In the main stream, some odd adventures which make the goal success of the prime character. 4. The main character's achievement in different manner and method. 5. The Choicest selection of the name of the main theme. 6. Wonderful variety of the sub-plots attached to the main plot. Acharya Anandvardhan in his book 'Dhwanyalok' he has given the following five topics to make the main theme extremely interesting:

1. Weaving of the main plot-may it be fanciful imaginary plot or it may be historical, but it should have been woven with the following 'Bhavas' - viz. 'Vibhav', 'Sthayibhav',

'Anubhav', 'And Sancharibhav'.

2. Even if the main theme is historical, leaving aside the awkward tendencies, to clinch to the main theme by resorting to fanciful ideological imagination, which would create a super sensation in the mind of the reader/observer.
3. Just not to follow the rules and regulations of the principles related thereto, there should be arrangement of re-establishing relations for the manifestation of the main interest - justification.
4. To crete the situation, to raise the sensitiveness, and calm down the unnecessary excitement although there may be adverse circumstances but yet to stick to the main theme and continue the interest.
5. Even if it is possible or not possible to decorate the subject matter with appropriate ornamentation and the like.

Tilliyard, Kuntak, or Anandvardhan - to keep all the three together leads to an idea as to why and how. The reply to this query is that if we judge the subject matter with an angle of comparative assessment, then the gist is very easy to arrive at, simultaneously, that whatever Tillyard has narrated in brief- according to time and space - the very theme - the very subject - the very idea has been discussed, analysed, criticised, dissected, digested by Kuntak and Anandvardhan - both - in a lucid, interesting mode and manner much earlier. Tillyard has emphasised on excitement and the impact thereof, and how to control the very same has been discussed by Tillyard in a very lucid manner. The traditional coverage of various incidents, events, sub-plots, has been so elaborate that it is beyond Tillyard to adjust to that particular situation. Although all the three agree on the main theme; but still there is little difference in individual approach, which makes the difference crystal-clear. Tillyard's observation is that the obliqueness of the stor is based on great expectation. Anandvardhan resorts to the Main interest 'Rasa' of the theme; Whereas Kuntak always stresses on the effective expression and he weighs his words in the same form, style, and planning. Anandvardhan has branded as Interest' 'Rasa' as the ironical-suggestive aspect and we have already discussed its definition in the beginning only. The entire 'Rasa-Sahitya' is incorporated by Tillyard in his oblique poetry.

The 'Interest (the main 'Rasa') of the Plot or the story, it is the oblique meaning which comes to the forefront lucidly, as has been manifested by Tillyard and as he expects. But even then there is some difference is there and it is this. Tillyard gives importance to the sentimental excitement, and he expects different meaning - his inclination is towards human feelings and not towards the thoughts of the theme. According to him the oblique meaning of the plot, according to Anandvardhan, the main sounding and suggestive thought, resorts to great expectations. Meaning to say the ironical meaning is the main aim. In the Indian poetical the 'interest', the .main 'rasa' is the only main matter of concentration and observation, but when Tillyard is referring to great expectations, this has already been discussed in the Indian poetic science. For example, in the 4th chapter of 'Dhwanyalok', Anandvardhan has drawn our attention towards the situation of Mahabharat and the oblique interpretation in the form of great expectations has been described by him as under:

'In this Mahabharat - the Great poetry - there is always praise for Lord God Krishna - the Vasudeva - only. He is highlighted every where, which gives us a conclusive conclusion that in the story of Mahabharat, the descriptions about the 'Pandavas' - is fine, at the end - goes into oblivion - this is nothing but the creation and mani - festation of 'Maya' - in reality, Lord God Krishna is above all the story - the plot - the composition - the theme, the narration all morality their existence compared to the creation of 'Maya' and as such it is advisable to attach your attention to the lotus feet of Lord God Krishna. In reality, one should not attach one's mind to the perishable worldly wealth, and one should devote his time towards, 'morality', 'winning' 'Bravery' all the virtues together or in any one singly, one should apply his mind, because this mundane world is useless, and store-house of miseries only. The oblique meaning is evidently expressed by these very words.

The reality is this that whatever Tillyard has tried to express, write, manifest in his writing, in his-sayings, establishing his views - all these have already been told/narrated/expressed by our ancestors in the past in a very lucid, simple way - this has also bearing on the Western culture also. Westerners, even before Tillyard, have commented upon, said their views on, elaborated in many different ways, the very version Tillyard has tried to express. In expressing his views in many ways, he is not driving at his originality as its own of course, that does not mean that we should not give credit to him for whatsoever he has done; we have to take into account his idea/ideology/views on 'Millers Tale' 'Lysides', where he has tried at a length to throw light on oblique expression, interpretation, meaning, etc.

**5. Characterisation**

Tillyard in his views and sayings has given more stress to the main story/theme than to the characters. what ever the characters say obliquely Tillyard says that it is due to the main story only. He too has even admitted that such possibility is always there. There may be a poetry whose oblique meaning is expressed through the medium of the characters, but still he is of the opinion that we should not give more stress to characters in comparison to the main story-theme. For oblique characters, he gives importance to class - society. According to Indian poetics, there has been three divisions, which have been considered important, viz. 1. Story, 2. Hero, and 3. the 'interest (Rasa); all the three have been effectively appreciated. Its originality comes before us in the 'Interest - Rasa' exhibited, and when the characters eulogize the idealism obliquely, the very characters emphasise the spirit thereof effectively. Vasudev Sharan Agrawal, in his book 'Charitra Nirman', he has correctly observed the character of Rama - the Hero of Ramayana. It is on account of these very oblique-meaning that the entire Sanskrit Literature is rich and so many editions of their criticisms have been published.

As far as there is problem of class-representation in our literature, it tries to interpret oblique-meaning in the best possible way. In Hindi Poetry, this is the modern - present age - development, which has nothing to do with the past at all. If we go on analysing the series of such characters, there would be endless such characters, such as 'Eklavya', 'Susharṃa', and 'Yudhishthir' which can be ascribed as -Untouchable shudra person, deserted illegal illegitimate child, difference of faith, and the incarnate representative of war, - all are impressive in their own way. In the vast enormous story of Mahabharat these characters have failed to solve the problems prevailing then; which problems have been evidently raised in this Pauranik Maha-Katha. If we critically analyse, we would come to a hoary conclusion, that the present day problems of this age, are the direct derivative of unsolved problems of those days - it is an oblique replica - an inverted version of gross negligence the then allowed in those days. In apparent they appear to be direct, but in reality, they are oblique - as oblique as they could be - borne out of frustration, dis-appointment, discontent, delusion.

The fact is that Tillyard has not been able to bring forth any serious topic about the characterization. He has tried all his efforts in establishing fact that out of the text, there is no image of the character. His this formula takes him away from his one formula established before about the characterisation. It would have been better if he had tried to establish some examples, where obliqueness would have been principle formula, but he has not been able to do justice to this - and in the prose field, he has been able to give only one example of 'Pickwick Papers'.

**An observation of Hindi Poetry vis-a-vis Direct and Indirect i.e. direct and oblique poetry**

In Hindi and Sanskrit Shlokas, we find many examples of oblique poetry as has been addicted by Tillyard. When a poetry has to be taken into consideration with the suggestion/the third sound, it carries, we shall have to remember Tillyard, who has made substantial efforts to prove his theory in this direction. There is no dirth of poetry void of 'Rasa' - there is ambitious assortment of each variety. But there is some problem in this. The poetry has very many varied critical sub-divisions, and the poetry has been written in the wide back-ground of Indian poetry. One cannot relish the beauty of this Indian valuable poetry, unless and until one has the sound barometer of understanding Indian delicacies of Indian Poetry. More of the poetry, which we come across, they are suggestive of a third meaning, they relate to various lady-like heroines, the odd and even circumstances, together with the involvement of the 8 'Rasas' exposed profusely. To be precise, for example, Indian Poetical science is full of variagated decorative illustrations - direct and oblique - suggestive and sincere, direct and indirect - there is no end to this epilogue; but then to relish it, to understand it, to digest, to criticise it, one has to have a full and detailed understanding of the big 'Shashtra' himself, without which the labour would be futile - it would be an exercise without any laudable result. To appreciate, one has to know - one has to have knowledge.

All the examples of'Dhwanyalok' and'Kavya prakash' are full of varied varieties of the best sort. Hindi poetry of the period of 'Riti' are also mainly of this type only. Poetry by Bihari are all full of suggestive sentiments, but then they are full of complicated, un-derstandable, incomprehensible series of comparisons, embellishment, decorations, such as 'Khandita Nayika', 'Anya Sambhogya Dukhita', 'Kalahantarita', 'Manini' - such varieties of leading ladies, then comes the question of meeting place and meeting time, girl-friends, atmos-phere leading to spring and environments, flying of birds, colour of natural greenery, the song of seasonal birds, all this ask for an understanding mind - on open mind. The irony in the poetry is a traditional outcome, outburst and it does follow the traditional line of expression. The poetry in Hindi, such as 'Chhayavadi Poetry', 'Nai Kavita' 'Akavita' - all these lead to a field of suggestion, in which there is a free atmosphere.

As far as the question of direct poetry is concerned, 'Nath' Sahitya 'Siddha Sahitya' and its secret-delicate-formalities and the jumbled (un-understandable by an ordinary human being, on accounts of its secretive quality) mumbo-jumbo, come into the category of Straight Direct Poetry only - there is no chance or scope of any indirect, or oblique interpretation on accounts of its peculiar existence, verification, composition, narration; It has one direct meaning only. But for those who are authorised to understand it. Examples can be given, but the time and space do not permit us to encroach upon the untilled subject.

The poetry of Jain Sampraday definitely they do not oppose the 'rasa' invention, but their tendency is always of 'Preaching'. It is to be observed that each writer has its own/his own speciality/peculiarity; with which he is naturally gifted. For Example, Amir Khusaro - his riddles and rhymes can be classified as 'Decora-tive/Descriptive' only. In Rasa Kavya, we find political policy matters only. In 'Bhakti' kal, Kabir and Tulasi both - their tune is direct and preaching. There is no dirth in Tulsi-style about 'Rasa', but then it deals with history only. Although in his sayings and compositions, there have been incorporated many great expectations. Whereas in the couplets of Kabir, it is dry flow of social situations. Although his irony is too strong and piercing, but they do not come into the category of oblique poetry, because its suggestive sense strengthens the main preaching subject. There are poets like Gang, Rahim Vrunda, their compositions their couplets, their sayings are incorporated as descriptive only. In 'Ritikal' also there was preference for 'Preaching-couplets' The political situation the then prevailing was responsible for this metamorphosis. Where as Tillyard covers all the present poetry under the roof of 'Oblique' poetry, which are arrived at by a laborious practice to create electrification in the readers.

Bharatendu-Yug is the time showing the mixed compositions but mainly they are descriptive only: narrative only. For historical time, we have to give credit to 'Dwivedi' - kal only. There is no dirth of 'Interest' and 'ornamentation', but yet, if we would like to praise the style, we shall have to reckon the names of Gurubhaktasinh 'Bhakta', Ayodhyasinh Upadhyay, and Maithilisharan Gupta for their poetry which is worth appreciation for its descriptive value. The creations/compositions by Gurubhaktasinh and Hari Audh, are equal to the style of Mathew Arnold. Guptaji can be called the 'Tennyson' of the Hindi poetry. Guptaji's fully having his wonderful exposition in his historical style. His poetries are the proven proof of his ability.

'Chhayavadi' is the time of the defeat of narrative poetry. This is time for 'Suggestive Sound'. Yes in this period we shall come across many pseudo poets who are nothing but an impression of artificial identity. This is the period of Shailey and Keats. When history is to be faced the power of the pen sometimes gets dis-heartened, because one has to stick to facts and no imagination on a run riot. In Mahadevi Varma, you will not find descriptive procedure but after the period of 'Chhayavad', there has been change in the value of poetry and thus meaning ful poetry came into beings, Progressive poet improved their style. But in this period, poets like Hari Audh tried his hands on 'Interest' and 'Ornamentation' and ultimately it remained a poetry by name only. But once the 'Chhayavad' was over, we can come across descriptive poetry with great esteem.

Vardhman, Siddharth, Tarakvadh, Parvati, Angraj, Bhumija, Senapati Karna, Krushna Charita Manas, Krishnayan, Urmila, Kaikaiyi, Queen of Jhansi, Haldighati, Jauhar, Vikramaditya, Jan-Nayak, Saket-Santa, - In all these poetical composition, the main 'Rasa' is 'irony' 'Oblique-identity' only, and their main style is Historical. In 'Lokayatan' also the beauty is that of the historical description only. But Urvashi, Anupriya, Andha Yug, One night of doubt - all these compositions are specimen of historical style and they are, in their own way, full of 'Oblique' expression, whenever necessary.

To-day's new poetry, 'A-kavita', 'Ajit' are the out come of the pressure of the present day movements and they are significative only. Language, selection of words, impression and unrealistic statement are the main reason for change in the poetical composition. But one thing can be categorically admitted that all these poetries have given preference to the 'Oblique' expression at its best. It is admitted fact that they have covered 'Dhwanyalok', mentioned 'Sup', 'tigant', and the instruments mentioned by Kuntal in his book, Parardh and Purvardh, : They have also tried to break the boundaries described by Tillyard, and they have used 'Irony' to establish the fact the world of poetry can not do without 'Oblique' Involvement in their expression, if they want to express their inner feelings.

**The Valuation of the System**

Tillyard has tried his best while evaluating his own critical system; he has tried to solve all the doubts about his motive, and by thus he has raised himself to quite higher standard. Tillyard has divided poetry into two sections - two divisions - Direct poetry and Oblique poetry. He has considered the 'Oblique poetry' to be the best of all; But he has also taken into consideration, the delicate difference in direct poetry - he has also taken into consideration pseudo/oblique interpretation and thus he has admitted that at other places also there is possibility of Obliqueness, at times. As has been told in the very beginning, that according to Anandvardhan, oblique poetry is 'suggestive' poetry; if we leave aside pseudo-suggestion, we still come across many specimen with direct or indirect suggestions and the specimen is 'Picture-Poetry'. Tillyard has modestly admitted in the individuality and universality of a poetry, and the difficulties arising out of them; but he has tried to reply that if the reader is of a particular special standard, then there is less difference in saying it with slant/Oblique; Thus this argument also does not impress the criticism in any way; The reader comes to his own conclusion. Still however, he admits that on account of criticism only, the capacity of the readers is trained; in his first impression, the reader does not come across the real meaning, as the poet wishes to convey, but when he reads the criticism which guides the reader and throws light on the real meaning of the poetry, he tires to understand the hidden-sense and enjoys the poetry more than when he reads for the first time.

Just like Tillyard, Anandvardhan in his book 'Dhwanyalok' has very forcefully tried to impress the fact that the criticism has its own bearing on the main poetry and he has discussed in detail with elite elaboration. In his 4th Canto in his 105 Karika he stresses that - 'In this way, when we take into consideration the view of 'for' and 'against', and with the division of sub- division, having taken into consideration 'the sounded suggestion', it shows the importance thereof; the personality of the poet takes a different turn altogether after following the trend shown by the 'Shastras', as to how an ordinary word also can 'suggest and 'sound' a different meaning as is expected to be translated.

Here 'Dhwanikar' has stressed his importance two-fold; he has tried to defeat those who have criticised his views, and he has set his own principles on proper guide-lines, and secondly, he has tried to guide poets how to eulogize one's ability and personality. As far as the first principle is concerned, Dhwanikar in the beginning of the book tried to emphasise what he wishes to convey. The three principles against the 'Suggestive- Sound method, 'Abhav-vad' (Not being there) Lakshnavad (the direct meaning) and 'Anirvachaniyatavad' (the philosophy of non- existent) have been refuted by him. He has hinted at all these three and then he has tired to re-establish the form of 'Suggestion-Sound', which he has already advocated in the past. In his first shloka he says that - We hereby try to establish the principle of 'Dhwani-Sound-Suggestion' which try to please the hearts of those who are sentimental individuals. Those who are well-versed with the deep meaning of the poetry, and those who value such 'suggestive-sound' long before, have considered and valued pleasurable, meaningful, soul of the poetry just like life existent; Some appreciate the absence of 'sound' also. Some have interpreted the sub-due 'suggestion' as irrelevant. Some have tried to attack the views, which consider that the expression by suggestion cannot be expressed by 'speech'.

The first karika of the book by Anandvardhan, is the proof of the fact, even before 1000 years, there were divisions in valuation of 'sound' and it was then accepted as a principle by Anandvardhan, and then he himself resorted his criticism to the principles of Poetry elaborately. The description of opposite principles and the refute by Anandvardhan to those attacks, is the proof of the fact that in those days of yore, the question of 'Sound' was a subject of discussion between 'Pundits' on this subject. But Tillyard believes that the people are familiar with the two forms of the poetry viz. Direct and Oblique, in one form or the other but it is he who made an attempt to make the principle formulation in egular manner.

> *"The distinction between 'Directly and 'Oblique' poetry is not new, and must be familiar enough in some form or another, but as an important initial criterion I doubt if it has been clearly formulated or consciously applied to critical practice.*
> *(Page 10)*

Now we have gone through the preface of both the books, and out of the comparison, one fact comes to lime light and it is that - the credit which Tillyard desires to have in this regard, cannot be allotted to him, because of several reasons. One is that there is game of a long time and the criticism are so very separate, that there is no chance for Tillyard to stand on. Again, it is very clear from the observation of both the prefaces that both the writers have kept the 'reader' in front of them: But Anandvardhan's main aim is to bring out the 'Intellectual ability' of the poet/writer in fore-front and thus he has tried to hint at 'Suggestion/Sound' of the poetry - the main aim is towards the slant meaning rather than the sincere reader. Here we observe that Tillyard has not paid any attention to the poet's ability and he has kept before him the reader and the critic and in fine he has given importance to the reader only. On account of this differentiation, there has been some change in the consideration of evaluation, which is very obvious. Tillyard has taken into account, the experience power of the reader and training in this regard, and he has given examples of many incidents and he has tried to give the oblique meaning of the poetry wherever possible. Although Anandvardhan has not that much clearly emphasised to train the experience-power of the reader, but still with his version, 'ten Broomah Sahridayamanah priteye' - we cannot deny his attempt in this direction., In Tillyard, 'Sahriday', there are involvement of both the type of readers. In the Book 'Dhwanyalok', Anandvardhan has emphasised the beauty of 'Teller' in such a powerful manner that we have in forefront a different image altogether, and in front of this image, the attempt of Tillyard in writing this book seems to be dwarfish. This is the reason, that with the help of 'Dhwanyalok', reader's digestive ability training is completely elaborated as nicely as it could be.

According to Anandvardhan, the poet has his own internal ability, and he has tried to rouse this spirit by means of instrumentation of 'Suggestive-sound' method, where the ability of the poet takes the form of end-less ability. He has elaborated this definition in his Karika 106 very clearly.

In the matter of 'Dhwani' and 'qualitative Irony', Valmiki and Vyas both the have corroborated that the speech and the reader - both are affiliated to the meaning and in this connection, they come out with an unimaginable beauty, which they obtain, out of the many qualities of 'Sound' Dhwani, if the poetry is embellished with only one quality; the old poet, with his speech, relates the meaning in such an impressive way that it bears a different form altogether and even the old meaning is turned into a very impressive 'Irony', which makes it more beautiful. Shree Anandvardhan has given four examples to prove and substantiate his theory to establish this new theory and new definition taking into consideration various main divisions and sub-divisions of speech, comparison, and ornamentation. Out of the outcome of the sound (Dhwani) the embellishment is so high that the people are impressed - their ordinary meaning is similar, but then there is absence of some special effect. Not only that but also Anandvardhan has given main stress of 'Rasa' - interest - and he has defined many big poetries like Ramayana and Mahabharata. According to Anandvardhan, this system advocates the interpretation of one single sentence into different ones according to reader's angle and understanding; it developed this capacity. This novelty is used in both the matters, by means of ironical words and meanings. When we touch the sub section of this irony, that too touches the same thing, but on account of want of time and space, relative examples are not specifically mentioned.

Now we touch the direct poetry. Tillyard says that this poetry cannot die - it is being written in large quantity and we can not ignore the importance there of. Anandvardhan has shown many ways to interpret one word into different meanings and he has shown several remedies and given several examples in his book. In his 11th Karika he says that -

The infinity cannot come on account of its ironical interpretation, but if you touch the reality, one can find newness in the meaning and to stress he has advocated may arguments in his books in favour of this subject. He says that even in direct poetry, according to position, country, time, there may be difference in meaning, which creates unlimitedness and it creates a novelty, and as such, on account of various sub- divisions, from one it seems multifold in understanding, meaning and substantiation.

Over and above the difference of time and space, there is newness in the subject and he has given many examples and he has admitted about common and special divisions and the quality of the poetry - and if one group does not believe the other group, and if one group criticises the other and vise versa, there may be an end less discussion. His Karika No. 112 reads as under:-

> *In the previous Karika No. 111, we have mentioned the difference about and of time, space, condition, which affects the composition, the words, the original meaning and the literal meaning, and the ironical meaning - we cannot just ignore the fact - the truth - the existence of reality.*
>
> *Very clearly, Anandvardhan and Tillyard, both have admitted categorically that direct poetry as important as any other and this sort of poetry is being written/composed in great number. Tillyard has said that -*
>
> *If man kind could reduce his poetical luggage to the omnibus volumes of hundred.percent master pieces and could both enjoy the volume and continue to add to it, the argument of scrapping statement poetry would be strong.*
>
> *(Page 109)*

This statement makes it clear emphatically that there cannot be always oblique poetry composition in front-fore and not that there can not be direct poetry without taste, and as such it should be taken for granted that the direct poetry will continue to be written, composed, and published and it will not lose its important position, in the past, present and future.

In fine, as matter of the final conclusion, we may arrive at a statement that the 'Oblique' poetry of Tillyard and Anandvardhan's 'Dhwanyalok' are the synonyms of the same subject, theme, theory and belief. Both have agreed that the touch of irony in the poetry is necessary, but nevertheless, they have also not set aside the importance of statement poetry or direct poetry - they have both openly admitted the observation. Anandvardhan mainly stress on the training of the poets and Tillyard's observation, stress, and importance is on the training of the reader's taste - but the main meaning of the sayings is the same. Although there is a time distance between the two- between Anandvardhan and Tillyard - there is a meaningful gap of 1000 years - but that does not mean that the importance of Tillyard is less in any way. There is intelligible, intelligent, and cosmic similarity in the statement of both - the vibration, even after years are lively and lovely and we given importance to Anand vardhan by quoting his Karika No. 115 in support of what has been stated before.

Time, space, position - there are such subtle difference which leads to the interpretation towards infinity, but yet there is similarity between the two poets, may be they belong to different countries, (Space) at different time/period (time and different conditions -war time, peace-time), etc. It is an unquestioned fact that the vibrations of the poetical geniality, ability to observation from a different angle, looking at a thing with a different angle, generally remain the same; What is said by Kalidas, is said by Shakespeare, what is said by Tolstoy, has been emphasised by Tagore - the time, space, distance become irrelevant and they are united with one bond, - they are all poets - flyers in the fancy of imagination - at their will, - 'Niyati niyam rahita....'. It is also astonishing to observe that two poets of different, space, time, and position, take up the same subject, and yet give the description in an identical, impressive manner. It is really un understandable, as to how this could happen. But the fact remains, that it is too true. We cannot doubt about any one about the repetition, at all, under any circumstances.

Similarly, what is true about poets, it is true about their critics also; There are poets with unquestionable personality, but there is equally critics of the same unequivocal standard, far above from ordinary standard - their main attention - focus is only the real beauty of the poetry; And we cannot but help confirm that both Tillyard and Anandvardhan are sailors of the same boat - they are part and percel of the same field - the same arena - the same ideology - the same humanism - reality.

Tillyard's dialogue cannot be said to be repetition. The difference between Tillyard and Anandvardhan is not only that of 'Time', but

'Country' also. His base is on primarily those provincial - occidental culture which are the basis of Greek. Latin, English and French Poetry. And it is this reason therefore that there is apparent considerable difference between the two valuation - which are unavoidable - and still they are natural. The Western will look at things with Western Culture and Western view point, whereas the ancient Indian or occidental poet will look at things with his own traditional angle which will be quite varied and away from both the ideology. It is a challenge, but then well accepted. A westerner has taken the trouble to have a peep into Eastern culture, studied, tried to digest it, compare it, with views and opinions of his side, and then formulated several formulas, for which we cannot but help him congratulate for his bold enterprise. He has tried to give out his own independent criticism and views and opinion. His Intelligence, memory, and poetic-taste - all are of excellent standard. He has studied the principle of poetry quite well, and then only he has attempted to undertake the enterprise, for which bold step, he deserves compliments and congratulations from those, who care and can to appreciate efforts of a Westerner. It cannot be ignored that he has selected the principles of 'Vakrokti' - Oblique-meaning and then he has published his views boldly - we congratulate him again and again, and humbly appreciate his efforts.

*Chapter VII*

# New Dimensions in Oblique Interpretation

In his Shloka 72 of 'Dhwanyalok', Anandvardhan has shown how the suggestive meaning can be sounded with the help of different formation of grammar and the language. He has given a full description on this subject in his 3rd chapter. Kuntak has also tried his best to criticise how grammar and its sub-heads would be in a position to help arrive at a suggestive sound; but then there 6 + 8 division - delicate differences - through the instrumentality of which one can arrive at a new condition. Six bhedas of varna Vinyas -

Eight Bhedas of Pad Purvardh Vakrata - viz., "Rudhi-Vaichatrya", 'Paryay', 'Upchar' 'Visheshana Samvrati', 'vruti', 'Ling-Vaichitrya', and 'Kriya Vaichitrya'

Six Bhedas of Pada Parardh Vakrata -

'Kal-vaichitrya', 'Karak', 'Purush', 'Upgraha', 'Upsarga', or 'Nipat'. In his effort to establish his principle, he has tried his level best to advocate how 'Oblique' interpretation could be accommodated with the help of the language. These sub-divisions, and references thereon are so wide, varied and delicate, the undoubtedly, the efforts of Tillyard in comparison to the foregoing, would be got dwarfed, howsoever sincere they may be. If we take into consideration, the modern trend in the literature, the explosion of new angle and tendency of thinking at. If we look at this with a modern out-look, we have before us - the problems of modern times, the changed out look to look at the poetry, non-acceptance of the view of only one 'RASA', as the final touch, International relations, the entanglement of the present-day situations and circumstances, science, and Psychology - all these problems to get the knowledge and try to solve them adjust them, and there has been so much of investigations and innovations in this science that a different structure, formation of the poetry comes before our eyes. In this the change in the language, continuous research, and one has tried to ease out the usage of 'Oblique' interpretation, that for a while, we are at a loss to observe and admit that the modern times has gone far ahead of Anandvardhan and Kuntak. In this chapter therefore, we shall try to discuss all the modern changes and varieties with altogether different angle and observation.

What is art ? It is and outcome of an impression from experience, which one feels from the bottom of his inner core of heart. for this message, one has to take the resort of some meaning ful formation, and then only he can compose the poetry. And that is why it has been possible for poets to take resort to the modern art and to reach the 'Ironical' 'Oblique' meaning of the ideas. Right from the direct meaning only, one has to catch hold of the 'indirect' statement, version. The modern day art has made a close combination of Sculpture, Idol, Picture, Music, and poetry - of all together and brought all of them very closer; which may have touched the thinkers also.

The irony of the poetry is an outcome of the original meaning of the poetry only. It is also proved that the direct meaning cannot be completely eliminated from the poetry nor it is possible to do so. But yet it has been observed that the direct meaning in the present day poetry is getting thin day to day. To-day's poetry is full of irony/oblique interpretation and that there is end of direct meaning. Either we accept this as a poetry or second alternative is to completely ignore it, because it becomes understandable. Just like the art of painting and sculpture, the art of poetry writing to-day has been quite different these days. Just as in picture, we cannot find the original idea, as in the idol, we cannot find the art hidden in it, similarly the present day poetry also do not present before us any concrete ideology or a subject; The poet wishes different, where as the meaning so suggested is quite different from the angle, with which the poet had composed the poetry. In order to impress the critic, the poet tries different types of experiments using different elements necessary for a composition, such as 'letter', 'Word', 'ornamental presentation of the words', complex composition of sentences, full-stop, half-full-stop, colon, point, stop, hyphen, formation of letters, formation of words, the poet tries to complete mission by any means and he gets successful in his efforts.

Here we give below some examples from the poetry of American writer Mr. E.E. Cuming; whose technique is undertaken by present day poets. (The examples given here under are taken from the Book of E.E. Kumings' which is published Harcourts, Brace and Company,

New York. The name of the book is 'E.E. Kummings, Poems 1923-1954. The pages numbers given in the example, refer to this book mentioned hereinabove.) I. A. Richards is of the opinion that the poetry presented before us is a vision. Whatever impression falls on the mind of the reader at the first instance, is the impression of the poetry. It may be true that first impression even, may not be real impression, but it is also true that it cannot be denied. Kummings is such a poet that his first impression is impressive and important and he tries his all the best to fulfill his mission of composing poetry in the best possible way. But the technique that which he has taken into implementation cannot be over-looked - it is not only presentable - to be seen only; it has its own meaning, even if it is heard. It has been full meaning of direct meaning and in-direct/oblique interpretation also. Ordinarily the medium, through which he tries to express himself are as under:

A. Sometime in one line – Poor But Ter — Page 232

B. " " Two " – fly<br>
Scorchbending them<br>
selves - U curv E, into — " 199

C. More than two lines - Darkness the<br>
hungry Star<br>
which will e<br>
ven to<br>
tallly jiggle — " 41-42

D. To split letters/ words by hyphen or even without that too to gives

space between them — Page 199

1. Anguish (climbing<br>
s-p/r-a-l<br>
and, disappear)

2. tWeNtY, fingers — " 182

*2. Between the words and word combination to put interval -*

In the poetry of Kummings, every word in his poetry carries an important meaning. Poetry can be taken into consideration in its right light only when it is written in an atmosphere, which the poetry wishes to impress/convey. Kummings leaves space between words, between lines - he leaves space between two sentences conspicuously, and by this technique, he wishes to impress the reader by creating a different impression of what he wishes to convey - just have a look -

A. Among
        these
                red pieces of
    day (against which and                Page 199

To keep vacant space between words in an orderly fashion is also an instrument of the style of Kummings: With the help of this technique, he creates an impression on the mind of the reader, the thing that which he wishes to convey, in a particular mode, fashion, style, individuality:

under, a locomotives pouring violets        (Page 133)

*3. Arrangement of more than one words/words*

By separating the sentence, by putting in between hyphen - space, or no space also, just like, as is done in Sanskrit literature, or in Hindi literature - this is a tradition in this language, and he has tried to copy it, or to put into practice the same style with a bang. English is not a language, where there is much usage of 'Cases' such as nominative case, accusative case, dative case, possessive case, etc. But in Sanskrit Language these are normally used. Kummings has tried to use the 'Hyphen' often to impress the combination of two words, two sentence, two ideas, wherever he has thought it fit to do so; He has tried to write without giving space between the words (as is done is Sanskrit language) - thus-

(i) eyes which never smile, one two three four five, pigeons ju-stlike that, blue and green, pat hands bang rag.

(ii) hopes, hard; feet (feet
f-e-e-t nowheregoingaLwaYs        Page 248

*4. The same word to be repeated with different angle, vision, presentation:*

Kummings has a peculiar style of repeating one word, or a combination of words, or small/Big sentences, with different letters, different tables, or mixing with different words; This has its own value in reading, and listening also; Two examples are given :

Old The (The president
The president of the president
of the) president of the
(united The president of the
United States The president of the
united
states of The president of the United States)

(Page 284)

Here the writer wishes to write (Old The president of the United States), but then seen how he has done it - in how many different forms in how many styles, - there is no explanation for this - this is just his style. First of all he has written the with a capital T. Then he has repeated the word president several times, with capital P also. In this way he has repeated the words 'United' and 'States' often times, and several places it has been started with Capital letters, whereas at some places in small letters. In fine, the words 'The President of the United States' he has written with suitable capital letters.

This has become his - Kummings - style to write the letters according to his mood and at times he has broken the trodden path and exhibited his novel style in quite different form: For example:

of
THuUNdeRB
loSSM in

Page 250.

*5. Use of Tables:*

In the poetry of Kummings, you will find many use of tables at various places; and he has made the series in such a novel way that one table is associated with the second table and so on. In the middle of the two tables, he creates such a gap that it is worth having a look at; He does not follow any principle of Mathematics, except we may term the writing as 'caprice' - a whim - to stand out himself out of many to show to the world that it is he and he alone, who has broken all the trends, and started a new line of writings and showed a path to the world, where so far no body has ventured to tread. His tables (1) are concluded without a start (2) He may close the table and start the poem in the beginning only (3) It may be that the table may start, but the poetry may not be there; we give below several examples of his fanciful creations, innovations, his originality - his convention-breaking creations - rather a surprise to a novice -

(1) applause page 393

(2) dying is fine) but Death Page 431

(3) When what huge stopping earth then silent is Page 361

Last

(1) Only one snowflake (and we speak out name Page 361

(2) (This is an example of the end of his poetry)
blue
(sleep I new
girlgold

At times he makes experiments in such a novel way that it is un imaginable, which way the curtain falls ? He breaks the words into two - sometimes in side, some times outside. Even before the poetry starts he will put a broken word at the beginning and then the poetry does not proceed further : sometimes the lines begin broken and he uses his style in many ways - see the example given below :

tilt-
ing
lyful
of)
(s
r
BIRDSBECAUSEAGAINS Page 301

*6. Different usage of the puncutuational signs in a peculiar way:*

Overthrowing all the rules and regulations of grammar, synthetics, style, etc. he used the punctuation signs - stop, full stop; half-stop colon; semi-colon, question sign, exclamation sign, equal sign, - to use them at different places, at his, will, is his style, about which none have anything to observe, say, comment: He uses these signs according to his own ideas, ; In a wonderful way, he flashes a full stop after each word, or semi-colon, or colon - he breaks the words into two divisions to put the signs as he pleases. Sometimes he uses the same sign several times; some times he used all the signs at one place only in a decorative way - we give examples in support of what has been stated hereinabove :

(1) emptied.hills.listen.
,not, alive, trees, dream (
ev:ery:whereas:ex:tend:ing:hush Page 298

(2) ji (

(3) deep calm deep
& ???? Ht ????? T)
jim, jimm who (holy alone) holy (alone holy)
; jimmy alone Page 326

(4) s:
A ,
v t,
o( ;d
;:a:
nCeda:Nci;ddaannccimn
: Page 309
: Page 338

*7. Overlooking/by-passing the rules of grammar, spelling, expression, etc.*

As has been told in the past, in order to emphasise his own sayings, Kummins, to fulfill his own wish, all the traditional rules and regulations are set aside by him, and he sets his own grammar himself. He changes the constructions, spellings, according to his mood, whim, and caprice. Not only for reading, but in writing also; he manipulates the letters into words and creates a chaos - attach a letter another and detach a latter from third - his style has no rules no regulations, no boundary, no limit, no transgression,: some examples of his marvellous manipulations are given below :

1 mmmooo (moon)
2 mooving (Moving)
3 bloomoon (Blue moon)
4 awal (all)

As far as his sentences are concerned, there are no head and tail about it - there is no verb and no serial order. He arranges his words in such a way that in minimum words, he could convey the maximum. He does not believe in grammar rules, so that a reader could get impressed one has to arrive at a conclusion by its phonetic usage only.

**To-day's poetry and its oblique-interpretation**

We have given herein above the over all style of Kummings, so that one would know his command over language, its usage, and how to use it at its best by symbolically superb presentation. There are several of his poetries, wherein he excels himself, above all others, by his different angle and presentation. His technique is his own. Please refer to the book 'Poems by E.E. Kummings', published by Harcourts Bras and co. New York - published in 1923- 1954 on Page 190, his 34th poem, and his poem on page 255 (poetry no. 45) - these two are with making a mention. He is hinting at his own specialisation, by - not his inner version or outer version, but sensational ironical sentiments involved in his compositions - on account of its depth, it takes us to sublimity. How he is succeeding in his technique - how and why - what he intends to convey, what he intends to propose, how his technique is helpful to him in arriving at - the beautiful result, we shall have to refer to Mark Twin's criticism made by him on the book of E.E. Kummings. The poetry which has been selected for criticism does not represent all his specialities, and simultaneously, they are the poetry of four words only, but the criticism of this will lead us to conclude as to why Kummings resorts to his peculiar ways of writings and compositions. It gives out the oblique meaning of each poetry. This poem is from Kummings 12th last collection - named - 95 poems - this is the first poem, written as under:

l (a
l e
af

fa
2
s)
one
l
iness

This poetry is less than a full sentence, and it appears that the words have met with an accident and as such they are scattered as they are. On the printed article, it appears that a mirror has falled down and all the pieces have been broken and fallen a ground. If you look at it, more carefully, you will notice that the out form of the poetry is sufficiently clear and in orderly manner. There are in all 9 lines and in serial order 1 - 3 - 1 - 3 - 1. There are only 4 words in this poem and as is with other poems, there is no fruitful meaning out of this but if we look at it deeply, it will take us to a special picture to impress us effectively.

This poetry is divided into two sections - two divisions -

(1) One is loneliness and the other (2) is a left falls. By these group of words, the poet wishes to convey that in his mind, there is a gap of 'solitude', which is significant of a falling leaf. He would have said in his version that the loneliness is like falling of a leaf or in the alternative, he feels loneliness, when he sees that the leaf alone falls from the tree, but the poet wanted to present the poetry in a different form, where with he can convey an idea through irony/oblique meaning or 'sounding' - Dhwani - about he desired to convey. Whereas this poem does not stress at any point about the 'aloneness' of the writer. Had the writer stressed this point he would have failed to create loneliness suggestively, but the construction of the poem itself is of such type that instead of taking us to loneliness, the impression is that of a fantasy of different land, where there is not iota of 'Loneliness', 'dead body of a leaf'. This creation is something solid, which can show us a meaningful interpretation for a novel experience.

First of all we shall go to route of the poem - we shall ponder over 'Loneliness'. Here the poet has decided to separate letter 'l' and then he has dissected the remaining section into three sections - one - ' and iness. Here the letter 1 represents the type letter 'I' and now if we take before us the form of letters, it will read one, one, one iness - if next ' is also attached in the series, the letter

' will appear for five times in this poem. Thus 'I' has been repeated five times. This represents singleness of I into loneliness and he reaches himself. One would argue that this sort of aplitting the word in such a delicate way does not lead us to a solid background - solid meaning, but then this is a research. In using the word in this way, there is no rise or fall of value of the word, but then the critics will see a different value is it and call it a coined word - 'Plastic value' - a new neurological word in the realm of understanding and interpretation. There is no seriousness of the word meaning; however the handling of the word has put exhilaration in it and it has become a symbol of showing pleasure derived out of it.

After that there are three words and 10 letters. These letters 1,2,2,2,2,1 are shown in a peculiar order. Just like the poem, the meaning is also full of surprise. Having picturised the fall of the leaf from the tree, he has picturised the situation and that is why he has composed the poetry in that falling order a/le/af/fa/ll/s - all the arrangements of letters starts with small letter and in the second line becomes from capital letters and again the last letter takes the form of small and the next line starts from small and closes on big f. A also comes in two forms - small and large - and then the piece ends with small s. n this category the word order rather letter order is in the following form:

*small big small small big big small big big small*

This arrangement of letters looks like the falling dancing leaf and shows its delicacy. In the beginning and end there are 4 steps. In this way the fall of the leaf is fully depicted as it should and the poem shines out with the complete meaning of the composition. The arrangement of the words, not only creates the scene of falling leaf, but also it has listening value also. The falling of leaf has been tied with a musical intention with a delicate delicacy. From le to af there is a long recitation and joins with each other. In the following lines also l,e or s, are repeated and they have been given proper place to stand on. It sounds a definite decision and it is full of strength of expression. When you recite the word leaf and its 1 of loneliness, it creates a cadence and the reader stand fastedly steps on loneliness once again. The letter s creates an impression of repetition and the last coming iness does not make s of falls shy with these two words in the poem there are long lines also and it creates a cosmos between the sound and the reading. Meaning to say these lines takes the reader to the beauty of the poetry and the experience he enjoys out of this.

So far we have discussed about the construction of the poetry only and now we would like to discuss the matter as to where does the poem leads us to: what is that matter that the poet has tried so hard, experimented so delicately the new ideology.

As has been told in the past, the poem creates a picturesque scene of 'Ioneliness' through the instrumentality of 'Falling of leaf' There is no doubt that the entire situation hints at 'solitude'; and the present day man, though in the crowd of present day order, busy with the atmosphere- and though within, he feels without completely 'alone'. His time passes into lonliness only. His daily routine of being alone, makes him away from the society; The falling of leaf indicates that the person is away from the society desperately and it is an emblematical symbolical death of his individuality or his being a non-entity in a social order. It is also significative that the falling of leaf, and the lonliness, points out towards the transitoriness of the life, and it explains how fruit less the life is But this experience is not the lost impact of this poem, but this is the first step of life. Had it been the last impression, it would have resulted into self-pity; but definitely the summarize of the poem is not self-pity, but to take the reader to a far world of fantasy, which would give him or would lead him to land of silence and solace.

The construction of the poem takes us far beyond the literal meaning. The leaf does not fall all of a sudden; it falls with a rhyme a rhythmatic swerve with a musical tone just an artist in a circus falls from the top in an acrobatic art. The circus-artist is so tuned with his daily chore that when he performs a particular performance, he just does think, he has no time to think, he just acts, and does what he is supposed to without thoughtful thinking, or practice; he does it and that is all. He releases his mind and body and the body does his performance as he has been used to do so daily non-stop. This is the point of 'Self-Loss'. In this very way, any artist, may be an actor or performer, when he reaches a stage of self-less-ness, he loses his individuality, he just becomes a performer and the poet here wants to make reader the experience of what he wishes to convey. It is just like the saying of the Bible that - Those who want to know themselves, should first of all get lost - they should completely surrender.

The falling of the tree-leaf in a dancing manner does not only make us feel an experience of self-less-ness, but the dissesction of the words in the poetry also lead us to the self same conclusion. l-one-l-iness - the word is broken into four sections, and when we reach the second, it leads to us a different stage of self-realisation; our mind joins the broken pieces and makes us feel the experience of that 'lonliness' which he wishes us to convey. Simultaneously we also feel that the experience of this separate blocks - iness- means one has to leave 'pride' a side and the real remedy for this self-realisation in only self-destruction.

This poetry does not lead us to self-less-ness, but it tries to make us feel - the experience of - being under such circumstances. When the poem ends, it does not create an atmosphere of grave platonic metaphysical situation, but lead us to the seriousness of death. About the last impact of this poem, Mark Twain says that - "The poem which ends in a scene of serenity, of unhappiness and death somehow resolved, explains itself ultimately in terms of that special self-forgetting which is utter humility. The movement of the poem has not been swift and rollicking, full of confidence in the possibility of human transcendence. It has instead, been slow, difficult, even severe, suggesting the hardown disciplined achievement of a tragic self- knowledge." (Page 26 E.E. Kummings by Mark Twain)

**Some Problems**

The definition of this poem clears that for the presentation of an oblique meaning, to-day's poetry deals with every letter, the mode of the letter, its place, the full usage of the word in a skillful manner, independent usage or mis-use of function signs and symbols. In the language of Anandvardhan, what is called the direct meaning or apparent meaning, has no place in the poetry of these days. But these poetries raise several problems about the interpretation of 'Oblique' definition about which Tillyard has raised this very question in his book, as under: There are two ways in which interpretation of obliquity my turn out to be valueless. Either it may lead to such hopeless divergences of opinion that it proves to be nothing more than the exercise of individual caprice, or granted sufficient conquity of opinion, it may not in fact heighten most people's appreciation of poetry.

"The first danger can be assessed by experiment alone. When a sufficient number of intelligent readers test as sufficient number of oblique poems by their own responses we shall know whether the game is worth playing or not. I think that success is possible with some poems read by the right persons in the right mood. (Page 111)

In to-day's poetry, where there is complex coalition of 'obliquity', there is no place for the second doubt raised by Tillyard. But the real question is that the first doubt stands before us with a mighty stand. It will not be out of place to mention here that the comments on Kummings poetry by Mark Twain are not alone; there are other commentators also numbering about three more. There is no similarity amongst them and to reach to the end of the 'oblique interpretation' seems to be an effort of an individual caprice - that is all. It is true that the present day poet is passing through a tumultuous tradition, and his experience is all the more various. Some times he is not in a position to catch it properly and he is not in a position to express himself effectively, as he should. His individual reaches that level that there is no topic at all. And the poetry of common people, remains up to a little few only. But the main question is that whether the heart of the poet touches the movement at all. Only by taking the support of the intelligence, it becomes numb and experience-less and creates a situation of magic. It is possible that few poets or some of them may resort to such untraditional path, but then we have not to think with the view of those only: We have to think about the real poets. Moved, touched, suffered, who want to find out a way for their amelioration and they try to find out a way of expression of his own experiences. There was a time, when taking into consideration the traditional valuation, we were resorting to new oblique interpretation, and used to set a new trend. There has been indication towards the direct meaning and the 'suggestive meaning' in the light of the interpretation by Anandvardhan. We cannot say to-day that in the present day atmosphere, Anandvardhan is true to-day, because to-day's poet will break all traditional traditions, and will try to infuse new oblique meaning interpretation by giving them a new light - a new sound - there is no dirth of such poets to-day. To-day's time has its own problems - local, physical, and mental, and the question has taken such a disproportion at proportion that he himself has been a subject of a poetry. He is important in direct-meaning also. To-day's poet resorts to oblique-tradition for supporting his own views. The main problem in to-day's poetry is about the individual justification. The element of sincerest has been liquidated, eliminated. In this we try to give below gist of Hindi poetry by Shyam Parmar, which may not be appealing to every one:

*It is better,*
*when you feel uncomfortable*
*don't try to undertake any trouble*
*believe it all to be trash*
*Don't weight it - don't measure it*
*don't run to recognise it,*
*leave the poetry as it is*
*Just as you leave the rest of the paper,*
*after reading the main head lines -*
*proceed or change the page -*
*may be some body else reads it -*
*truth is that it is he who catches the truth out of it*
*and he tries to mix his darkness with my darkness*
*it is he who comes nearer to my poem.*
*(Poetry - out of the poetry - the reader of darkness -Shyam Parmar*

*(Page 38)*

About this poetry, Tillyard has said that 'Right persons in the right mood' and if we definite this, right person, is he who has had the experience of the turmoil and the right mood is his mental situation, where he tries to make research in to-day's context. But the problem does not end here. Two questions are raised. One is that the reader may take out the meaning of the poetry, according to his state of mind and if it suits his own end-interpretation - if the meaning suits his own individuality.

Whether the poet desires the same impact on him - he just does not care. Then there is no importance of poetry being objective. For the poet it is important because he has written the poetry, in particular mental situation and the reader takes out the meaning according to his own mental position and standard. The poetry can be important then only when the writer and the reader both are in the same mental condition. Over and above this there are critics who take out the real meaning out of it, only according to their own individuality and their own interpretation.

In reference to do-day's poetry, I would like to raise one pure question. Dr. Nagendra has tried to establish the fact that - may be Anandvardhan and Kuntak - have their own view which they would like to convey, but their stress on the 'Gist' and the importance there of in the poetry cannot be over-looked, because they both agree to establish the same principle, which they would like to stress and support. On this very point, they have tried to reply categorically that - it is the 'Rasa' only, which is the 'atma' of the poetry. There is no doubt that they both have agreed that the experience of 'Rasa' only - the experience is arrived at, on account of the existence of 'rasa' only. On the strength of this experence only he has replied to the question of to-day's poetry. But it has been observed that the poet does not take into consideration 'rasa' as the main factor nor does the poet think on that line. He is not alive about 'Rasa' and its importance. By chance, if there is one who would like to comment on the poetry of 'Kummings' on the basis of 'Rasa', may be he would tie it in the meaning of 'Rasa Chakra', but that cannot be said to be justified. 'Rasa' is not the only measurement of to-day's poetry, and hence to look at it is using a wrong measurement in this direction. The descriptive poetry has changed its trend with a speed, where the quality has become a thermometer of the mental balance/imbalance of the writer, where the writer tries to fight with te Society with very many problems and on the strength of his own conscientious souls alleviation, he tries to find out about himself. And definitely, his mental awakening is miles away from the 'substance' called 'Rasa'.

To-day's world is changing; and it is just impossible to take resort to any subject matter, we cannot set any measure-meter, when the change is so rapid and in fluid state that it is not possible to decide either way. But regarding the construction, we can say without doubt that whatever turn the poetry may take, it may be involved with many changes, but for experience and its definition, 'Dhwani-Siddhant' it the only principle, on the basis of which it can win the laurel. Definitely there is no importance of the sub-heads of 'Dhwani' as announced by Anandvardhan, but then suppose some such writer like 'Shyam Parmar', through the medium of his poetry, wishes to reach him, and then when he reads out his composition, he will reach a particular levél where suggestive element would be there - it may not be in the form of 'Rasa'. His formation will be due to disturbed situation of his mental state; not in the form of creation of 'rasa'.

In to-day context, looking at the present day situation of 'poetry', there is no possibility of creating some new version of 'Dhwanyalok' nor a new book can be written. The reasons are many. But, in fine, if we conclude, that in the present day context, if there is any scope of amelioration, it is on the basis of 'Dhwani-Siddhant' only.

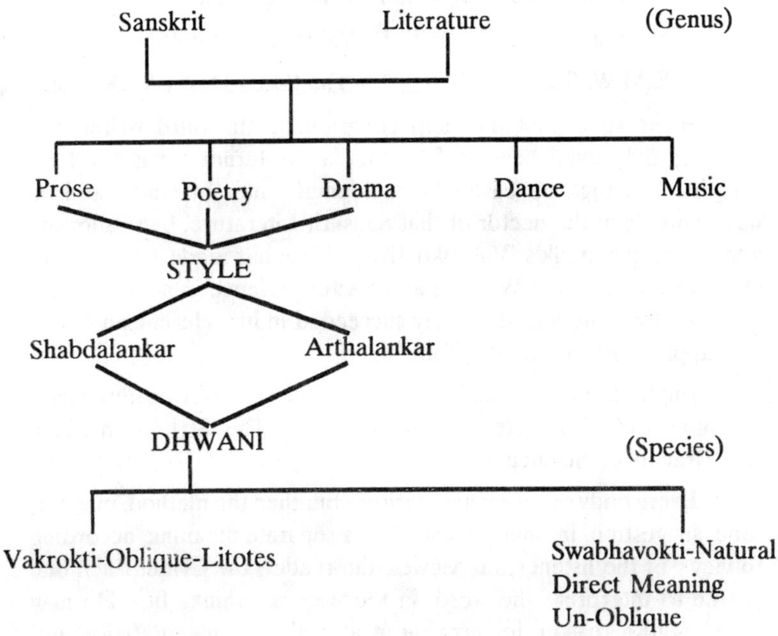


There are many divisions, and sub-divisions - can be said to be innumerable.

Then there is - comparison - Metaphor - Figures of Speech - these are also of innumerable types.

Then comes the science of Decorations/Ornamentation and the meaningful the interpretations - according to views point of the viewer/critic.

Each details would need individual independent elaborate chapter to give full justice to the statement, explaining the possibility of the interpretation arrived at.

Oblique - Litotes - saying is coming from the words "Vakrokti" - Slant saying - : the speaker speaks, but its interpretation/meaning/Irony is decided by the listener/reader/the critic: Here we give only a bird's eye-view of an Expanse.

There may be many, but here we discuss only 3 big figure-heads -

Anandvardhan - the writer of 'Dhwanyalok' -

Kuntak - " " " 'Vakrokti Jivitam' -

E.M.W. Tillyard - " " " 'The Poetry-Direct & Oblique'.

Here we cannot but help congratulate the third writer, viz. Mr. Tillyard - who being a foreigner, a westerner - has tried his very hard to pick up eastern - occidental - literary study, and he has drank deep the nector of that Sanskrit Literature, by swallowing and chewing Kuntak's 'Vakrokti Jivitam'. He has made a Herculean effort to compare the Western and Eastern science in a very critical view point and he has definitely succeeded in his Herculean effort. We appreciate the great effort.

But before we proceed further, we shall have to critically analyse the subject of 'The System' - 'The Method' - The 'Style' - on which this Branch of Science is based.

Every body says - speaks - writes - but then the method, manner, tone, suggestion, intonation, each has a separate meaning, according to views of the listener, the viewer, the reader, the Critic. Each one is free to interprete the word, in the way one thinks fit - He may have his own reason, for arriving at a particular interpretation and may be - he may be justified - one may like the resultant comment or not.

Let us have a detailed bird's eye-view of the science of Stylistics. The importance of Style in Sanskrit Literature - a study - 'Indian Poetical Literature' in Sanskrit' is a vast ocean - it is a seam-less sea - there is no beginning nor end. In English language the word is 'Stylistics' which is quite popular among the literary circle.

We come across many examples of different styles, forms, direct and indirect, in all the Branches of Sanskrit literature, for example, you can come across - this cross section - in Prose, Poetry, Drama, and each one is looked at, observed with an angle of vision, the reader the viewer, the critic has - There is a saying that 'A man cannot see in another man, more than what he has in himself." For example, for appreciating the effort of a 'Research Student' - only another student of a higher level would be needed to evaluate the efforts of research scholar. Research Scholar cannot be critically analysed by a 'Rustic' - an illiterate person - unconcerned with the depth, the beauty, the elegance the literature contains. 'The Style' cannot be a monopoly of one country or province or a country. Westerners too have full command over their language and we have come across thousands of examples of their taste and study.

We admit that the subject is quite vast - with 70mm vista-vision and we shall have to make an effort to arrive at our observation.

The language can be divided, classified in two categories, primarily - The first is general language of the common people, and the 2nd one is that of poetic, the decorative, ornamental, impressive language. There are nine elements in this science and they are :

1. Trangression/diversion
   - it may be due to grammar,
   - " " words
   - " " meaning
   - " " rules
2. Parallel Construction
3. Ambiguous interpretation
4. Irrationality & Paradox
5 Difference in Linguistic Structure.
6. Structural economy
7. Onomatopeoia, Rhythm, Pause and Rhyme.
8. Non-contextuality.

The poetical language and its elements (Style + system) The main feature of this science is its observation on the writer's 'Style' - the science based on this is called stylistics. The style may be of hundred types; how to live in style; the style of food - habits, the style of writing and speaking - but here we are to take into consideration language style. It may include both - or many - speaking - writing etc.

Two persons may tell or write on the same subject, but the style of both may be quite different. The one would express in a very simple language, whereas the other man would say the same thing in a flowerish/impressive way. May be one be educated whereas the other may be a rustic - a villager - an innocent person without the knowledge of any books - a man who had no opportunity to go to school. The sayings of the uneducated may be, for a while clumsy, un-understandable and informal, incomplete and uncanny; whereas the language of the 2nd one, who is quite educated will express himself systematically, absolutely clear and in an understandable manner. The under-studied man may not be able to convince the listener, because in his statement, he would not be coherent, but the 2nd one will be in a possible way, he may impress the listener effectively. To be precise, every one, each one, out of a group will have his own style and no one man's saying would be identical to another; everyone has its own way of expressing himself - he thinks that he gives a good version of what he has seen is the only correct version; whereas the other man's version on the same subject would be totally different - although meaning the same. That is why Dandi in his book Kavyadarsh 1-40, has stated that 'there are many ways of speech with various different expression.

And here comes the reason for this variation; We have to take into consideration, the mental state of the speaker, and also the education standard - how far he is educated; whether he is only school educated; college educated or higher. Not only that but also, the Speaker's position in the family, society, the environment in which he has been brought up - environment of a city, environment of a suburb, a denizen of Zuggizompadi - each will have its impact on the version of the teller. It is all the more important as to what educational standard he has reached. A school drop out will have his say according to his education, whereas a University Graduate or any one else, will have his say in somewhat different sophisticated manner. Over and above all these, more depends upon the teller's own style; Whether he is a fast speaker, or a slow speaker, a superfluous, or a person with a deep study, all these again go a long way in expression. Thus there are two different branches of this science - One (1) Once own - internal - this is main - and second (2) outer influence, which is dependent on the former. When we stress that 'Personal own' - it means his own basic mental and intellectual status/standard, which he gets with his birth. Thus a boy with a silver-spoon in his mouth and an ill-bred brat will look at a thing in quite a different way and express accordingly. One may say that it is God's gift, or one may have a peculiar style as a legacy from the parental - mother-father's aptitude/attitude or by once more step, we may call it that he may have arrived at the culture on account of the status of birth of this life, or if we go beyond, life from the previous birth. The body elements too play an important part in this. Whatever may be, there may be one element, there may be more than one element, or a combination of all the elements - the impact may due be to any other element, other than those narrated hereinabove. The mental and intellectual standard of each one is quite different from each other - one another. The world is full of number of people - hundreds, thousands, in millions, but it is interesting to observe that each one's standard is different from the other. It may be good or bad, balanced or imbalanced, developed or undeveloped or underdeveloped - out side agencies like the society, schooling, training, each counts in carving out a figure of each and every one. It is on this basis that the speech is born from the combination of one or more factors mentioned herein.

This particular peculiarity of the style is observed at many places, such, (1) In the speech, a speaker delivers on the platform, or (2) in the art of delivering a lecture by a professor, but also in (3) poetical compositions composed by different types of poets. Ordinary language delivers its ordinary meaning - in the eye of the speaker, and on the strength of the listener, the meaning is very simple and whatsoever has been told or said comes in a lucid language. When one describes a lady's face as good, her hand has delicate, he means it, he does not take the cover of any comparison, or allegory. He does not compare the face with the moon, nor does he say that the hand is as delicate as lotus

But apart from the ordinary versions, when a poet takes the resort of a poetic language, - it means a deviation - he distracts his statement from the ordinary meaning to a special meaning or a narration, he establishes the language on a higher pedestal - a scene to be seen by a common man.

Here at this stage, it is interesting to observe that on the strength of his poetic skill, one poet describes a subject as a particular model, whereas a second poet, will select the same model or subject, but he will describe in his own peculiar method or manner - and the difference of these two versions, according to the Indian poetic science, is the inner 'intellect' (Pratibha) of the poet. His capacity and command over formation of a poetry. Indian Professor Kuntak the great Acharya - has described this 'intelligence' in 3 phases. (1) the first is delicate natural exuberance - in sanskrit, it can be termed as 'Sahaja'. Quite ordinary. Whereas the other (2) quality would be quite different from the former - it may be decorative (preference to exhibition) which is branded as 'Vichitra' and the 3rd one is what is called 'Mixed' one, called 'Mishrit Shobha shalini' - an admixture of both the styles - simple + decorative - both.

Over and above this, as has been already said in the past, it also depends on various other factors - such as - family/upbringing/social circumstances/education - all these go a long way to describe Indian Poetical diversion - a poetical style, which also depends on geographical topographical divisions. Bhamah and Dandi both have branded these their style as 'Vaidharbhi' or 'Gaudiya'. Vaman has considered 3 phases - (1) Vaidarbhai (2) Gaudiya and (3) Panchali. There are other writers such as Rudrat, Agnipurankar, and Vishwanath, - these people have included amongst them one more division viz. 'Latika' - to telling four. Bhojraj believes in two formations, viz. 'Avantika' and/or 'Magadhi'. It is evident that these names relate to geographical zones, meaning writers - denizens of these provinces - places, who have a peculiar style of expressing themselves in a particular mode or manner. That is the reason why the style of the poet is branded as a style of a particular geographical division. But even then it is quite possible that the poet of one province, may not write in the style of a different province and may be true in vice versa also. But then all said and done, there is impression of his own intellectual level and education - and this helps him compose in either style according to his capacity. (Bharatiya Kavya Shastra (Pages. 399-403) denomination of styles)

The Poets - on the basis of his own and traditional circumstances and the resultant composition may be quite different by both the writers. There is a wide different angle in their expression. On the basis of the very selection of words, its compositions, and the structure of 'Padas' or sentences, or to say in the evolution of language - this is the basis of the selection of poet of a particular geographical province. This is the difference of one's style. When more than one poet takes up the pen, each one flies according to his own fanciful ideology, which gives the different forms of styles.

Let us take a next look at the writings of several other writers. For example the style of Shree Ved Vyasa. We just cannot dare comment on his style. On his names are Mahabharat and the entire Upanishads - all poetical narration. May be the generation of each poet of the next generation, went on adding to the main stream. We wonder how long this process was lasting - for an indefinite innumerable number of years. We now refer to a long list of ancient writers - such as Valmiki, Kalidas, Ashwagosh, Bharavi, Magh, Shreeharsh, Bhatti, Amaruk, Jayadev, such like poets. Dandi, Bhanbhatta, Subandhu - all the prose writers - Bhas, Shudrak, vishakhadatt, Harsh, Bhatt Narayan, Bhavbhatuti, - such like dramatists - all these writers have their own peculiar style in their writings - the distance is very clear.

Some use very simple words, whereas some uses far-fetched, un- understandable words; Some one uses long winding sentences; some unusual peculiar formations of sentences; some one loves long "Samasas"; some one uses difficult 'Tigants' or 'Thaddhits'; some one tries to push new style of the usage of a particular verb- form or grammar, to impress upon the readers, how knowledgeable the writer is; he is out to teach grammar in his own way and style; some one uses very simple, lucid language; some one forms out neology - creation of new words - some one has faith on the usage of old adage and old words; some one sticks to old metaphors only; some try to show out the mental psychological status of their characters; some one makes them just mechanical; so that the character would move on their balance-wheel; some one says his version in few words only, whereas the other wides his vista to 70 m.m. (Some story-writers use the style of Vyas - the style of elaboration) where as others use the style of 'Sutra- Shaily', meaning to say maximum in minimum words, which is very difficult. All these are formations of the style of a writer.

It is on account of these peculiar specialities that the readers having come across a particular line or a passage, at once, they would judge that these compositions are those of particular person; and 100% their presumption comes to truth. The reason for this clear cut decision is that every poet has his own peculiar (un-attempted - very simple - very normal - absolutely lucid -) style of writing - it is his own speciality - no attempt has had to be made to arrive at particular style - it - the writing flows very normally. This is the gift of gab; gift of the God. That is the reason, why a composition of one poet, does not talley, with that of the another; Both have their own angle, vision, and they both differ in their expression, out-look, elaboration, imagination. One cannot copy the other - that is again a beauty of the writing style. Alliteration comes to him normally; whereas the other would end his composition with a peculiar rhyme, which everyone cannot practice.

Thus when we emphasise on the 'Style', we stress the mode, the method, the manner, the manipulation, which gives a rise to a peculiar 'collection of words', 'Peculiar sentence', 'Peculiar expression', which are his own. The 'Science of Style' is termed 'stylistics', which means very clearly that the science which deals with the subject, having taken into consideration various aspects of the subject; we shall deal with the subject, elaborately, sometimes ahead, at an appropriate time and space. It is sufficient to stress once again that the style is the 'Identity Card' of the writer.

**Now we touch the topic of 'Language' and the 'science of Style'**

Westerners have confirmed that 'the literature is the creative use of language' - it is an experiment of expression in a particular mode, method and manner. It is the individuality of the poet, which is exhibited in his woven pattern of the language, which is adjusted to the thread of the subject, well- programmed, well-drafted, neither more nor less, neither tall, nor short, neither wide, nor narrow - all these creations, compositions are called poetry/poems, Literature, etc. Having taken into consideration all these factors, then the critic comes into the arena, and having taking into consideration, the peculiar usage of forms, he arrives at a conclusion, which can be summarily called 'Literary Stylistics or Science of Literary styles or in short it can be designated as "STYLISTICS" only. In the western literature this is a special knowledgeable subject of studies and it is accepted as a form of the language; Turner has termed both these heads as under: Linguistics: This is that science which analysis the fabric of the language and tries to show - how the language works. Stylistics - Under this various poems are critically examined, having taking into consideration, factors necessary to arrive at a conclusion, because this is scientific study based on several principles and policies. It is not a study at random. In arriving at a conclusion, many points are taken into consideration; On the language, on the form of the language; how the subject has been handled - whether it is palatable whether it has bearing the subject; whether its dimensions are based on the poetical delicacies, and this is the reason, why the stylists is considered as a Branch of the Linguistics.

G. N. Leech says - Linguistics and the Figures of Rhetoric - (Essays on Style and language - edited by Roger Foweler - p. 136). G.W. Tumer in his Stylistics Page 7 - says - 'Linguistics is the science of describing language and showing how it works."

In order to confirm this, Kuntak has accepted the principle of 'Ling Vakrata' in his book Vakrokti Jivitam 2.79, where he discusses about the peculiar delicacy of the point raised by him. This is in connection with the stylistics to understand this particular formula. 'This Mountain edge is disturbed due to heat and that is why I understand that the rain is expected which is going to out-do the domain of Moon and the moon-beam, and having taking the purview of the whole world, it will takes a form of winning the hearts.

Here the use of word 'Rati', in place of 'Tat' is significant of obliqueness of the suggestion - it suggests about the erotic Nayika, which will be met by the nayak called 'Megha' and hence it is branded as 'Ling Vakrata'.

Whatever 'Obliqueness' is concealed in this composition can be discussed further -

(a) In the eyes of Stylistics, this entire formation is composed having taken into consideration the word 'Tati' (Feminine gender) bearing in mind that 'Tati' is a female form in the form of a 'Nayika', To cool down the heat of the imaginary 'Nayika', 'Nayak' Megha will come and drench the 'Nayika' to her heart's content.

(b) In the eyes of 'Shailivigyan' - Stylistics, the attention of the reader will be attracted towards the feminine usage of the word 'Tati', because the word 'Tata' can be used in all the three forms viz. Masculine, feminine, and neuter gender, and that is why they have specially used the word 'Tati'.

Therefore the Stylistics is that part of Linguistics which concentrates on variation in the use of language, often but not exclusively, with special attention to the most conscious and complex uses of language in literature. (Stylistics p. 7)

Now next question: Ordinary Language: Language of the Poetry: & Style. In the light of the poetry, to understand the style of poetry, one will have to first study the 'Kavya-Bhasha' Poetic language: in this connection, we give below some examples, by way of samples:

**First**

Thou sittest - you sit here - please accept the seat. Please occupy this seat: This is your seat please, it will be comfortable, if you will kindly occupy this seat.

According to the standard/status/age/profession, of the speaker and the listener, there would be different usage of words in speech or poetry: The ultimate aim is to 'sit', but the way in which it is expressed differently, in different ways, by different people, is worth marking - noting. The same very 'sit', but how it is expressed ? This method of expression is called 'Style'. It is on the strength of this that different sentences, carry the same meaning of 'sitting'. It is quite different, according to each speaker - it contains, Order, request, respect, irony, insult - all these expressions come under one roof and that is styled as 'style'.

**Second Example :**

In sanskrit language for the expression of this style, they have given two examples - 'Shushka Vrukhsa Tishtati Agre' and 'Niras taru vilasati puratah'. The first sentence is harsh, whereas the second one is delicate. The critics have appreciated the second one very nicely. In order to express the position of the tree, the first sentence looks dry while the second one shows desired delicacy. And the reason for this difference is termed as 'Style'. In first sentence the vowels used are harsh, whereas in the second sentence the vowels used are 'soft' and that is why the effect thereof is also soft. The composition/constructions, and the 'samas' 'Sandhi' coming up in each sentence also carries weight. This is only a sample example; there may be many of this very type, where by using the delicate words, delicacy automatically prop up. These expressions exhibit the mental balance of the speaker; how one presents the same sentence, under the same situation, in a different mode, method, manner and mannerism. The state of the situation is the same; but how it is expressed ? To utter sentences in such a way that there cannot be a change in it. This is also a part of the style. This is the 'Style-base; according to stylistics.

**Third Example :**

Please refer to the drama 'Mrichha-Katika', wherein Shakar tries to exhibit his love towards Vasantsena (Book Ref. 8/18) where he says to her:-

O Lady with wide eyes, with ten sharp nails, pure white teeth adore you, you have a beautiful body. I fold hands before you, I fall at your feet, I am your servant; if I have behave in any offending way, kindly excuse me, please.

*'Eshah Patami Charamyo-vishalmetre'...... 'Tavasmi Dasah'..... (8/18)*
*Whereas to her Charudatta says that-*
*'Sada Pradoshi mam Yati Jagratah.......*
*'....Mamadya Shokantakar Pradoshaka.....' (5/37)*

'Darling - I spend my first night half, awakening, and the whole night is spent sighing. Oh lady Vasantsena, whose eyes are so beautiful, now if I meet you in he evening, it will remove, all my miseries.

It is evidently and abundantly clear that in both the proposals, there is a difference between the sky and the earth. The style is entirely different and there is some sound reason for this change. For example, the individuality of both the speakers, their social status, their family status, and their different taste, and mental embellishment.

**Now 4th Example :**

'The sun is rising'. This is a very simple, normal daily spoken statement. It is said/expressed in our daily, monotonus routine language - our day to day language - and still however, such phrases are used daily in our day to day usage.

When it is said that 'Sun is rising' - it means many meanings and one of it is there is a slight light in the eastern sector, but if the self-same sentence is to be explained in the scientific language, it will run like this - Because the rays of the Sun are slanted and perverted, they are being reflected and on account of its expansion there is some light being seen on the horizon, before the actually sun has risen. This is indeed boring, but that then that is an expression, translated literally due to its scientific version. Sentence is quite an ordinary one, but it carries many fold interpretations. The very same sentence - 'that the Sun is rising' is being manifested in the following manner in the Rigved:

*"Esha Divo Duhita Pratyadarshi Jyotirvasana samana perstat.*

*Rigved. 1.124.3.*

The mainen 'Usha Kumari' having put on the clothes of light - dress, it is being exhibited in the east and it reveals her own self wonderfully.

Usha is compared to a dancer, who in her charming clothes, undoing her beauty and it shows to the world the wonderful atmosphere - she is distributing light for the whole of the world. He is opening the darkness, just as the Cows opens the door of its shed of its own.

There is one more Rigved Richa -

*"Adhi Peshansi apate.... Navrajam vyusha Avarthanah. 1.92.4."*

"The sun is rising." this very version has been manifested by an English poet as under:

*But look, the morn in russet mentle clad*
*walk o'er the dew of you high eastern hill.*

*(Linguistics and Literature page )*

Meaning - 'Please have a look, how Usha in her un-clear clothes, (Just like a village folk) right on the eastern horizon, she is putting her steps on the dew drops slowly and steadily.

Now an ordinary sentence 'Sun is rising' - the words expressed in an ordinary routine common language have been beautifully woven in Vedic and in English language, according to the taste of the poet - the writer - and he has converged the wording in such delicate tasteful way by resorting the beauty of 'Style'. This very style is branded in poetical language as 'Kavya Bhasha meaning 'Poetic language'. Thus the equation is this -

Ordinary language + Poetic style = poetic style-language.

1. Thus the daily used language expresses the same meaning, but in a different manner - this is change in the style. (Thou sittest - Please oblige us by undertaking this seat) etc.

2. What ever is expressed in the poetry - may be - may not be there an admixture of imagination, but still the different style will bring forth different expression, such as 'Shushka Vriksha' and 'nirasa Taru' ..... Usages.

3. Common Language and/or Scientific Language, both give the same meaning, but in a different manner/style. In includes or does not include poetic imagination. There is difference/change in the style/expression. Just as we have already seen above in such examples.

Thus when we conclude the topic, we may come to conclusion that the self-same wordings or meanings can be said, expressed, manifested in different forms and manners due to difference in 'Style'. Of course this beauty of 'Style' is always there, and it depends upon person to person, who expresses and in what manner and method. Thus the usage or currency of the Style is not one, but having many varieties, according to each individual and his surroundings. And thus we again arrive at the same conclusion that 'Common language + 'Style' = Poetic Language.

*Even then this requires elaboration and it can be further discussed as under :*

Common language means day to day language, which is spoken and understood by a common man - a labourer, an artisan, a worker. This language is self-emerging. No one has to labour for expressing his language in a simple manner. It has no rules and regulations. grammar helps the language; and language fits in the grammatical formation, and it develops into a different mode/method/manner and there is change in each step, it grows, and the rules and regulations of the grammar get themselves changed into the new formation, according to circumstances - environments, atmosphere. It is however interesting to observe that the world's entire work is based on 'common language' and not on the 'Poetic Style'.

> *'Writing is a special, careful, elaborated, shuffled, pruned and tidied form of a language.*
>
> *(Stylistics p. 8)*

'Style is understood as an emphasis (expressive, effective or aesthetic) added to the information conveyed by the linguistic structure, without alteration of meaning. ('Criteria for Analysis of Style' Riffaterre, Michael in 'Essays on the language of literature' by Chatman and S.R. Lavin). And now comes the views of the critics. Kavya-Bhasha is that form which has been made up of Common Language + Style, but then the critics believe in their interpretation that 'on the whole', the language is the same. Lakshan of a Kavyabhasa is the same as that of the common language. The main reason for this version is that the style, which is a part and parcel of the Kavya-Bhasha, it raises the language from the base ground to a higher level, it makes it fly high in the air; meaning to say it infuses life in a statue. And hence the 'Kavyabhasha' is said to be the style' of the writer. We can translate as 'we have eaten your salt' - this has been used for the minute quantity of salt used in the food, but the whole food has been termed as 'salt'.

"A current definition of style and stylistics, is that structure, sequences and patterns which extend, or may extend, beyond the boundaries of individual sentences define style and that the study of them is stylistics."

> *(Poetry and Stylistics, Archibald A. Hill in Essays on the Language of*
>
> *Literature P. 389)*

Thus, in fine, we have observed that the formation of style has been styled into two different angles:

1. Common language (Or any form of language) is admixtured with an extra poet - Emphasis - and this is termed as 'style'. As we have observed in the version of 'Riffaterre'.
2. That the Common language (or any form of language) is added with emphasis or 'style' and the combination of the two becomes 'Kavya Bhasha' as has been mentioned by Hill hereinabove.

For example, if we see with an Indian Angle, when one says that 'the face is beautiful' is a very simple common language example, but when it is added with 'Metaphor', an addition of one word only - it makes the difference. When it says that 'face is beautiful as Moon' - this version enters the periferi of 'Poetic' field and it is branded as 'Upama Alankar'. In the words of poetic expression, this is a 'poetic style'. If we go tar and add few words more - 'Smaran' alankar - we may quote that 'Having seen the moon, It makes one remember the face of the beloved'. This is the formation of 'Smaran-Alankar. In Stylistics, it is poetic language.

Now the question comes about both the sentences which are poetic and it raises a point, what is the position of 'alankar' ? The reply to this point has been given by Anand vardhan that the ornament is a part and parcel of the poetry. It fits in on any part of the body. Shabda + Earth = Kavya-body + Alankar = Kavya. The self same version is that of Riffaterre. If we add 'Style' in common language, it becomes poetic language. Kuntak has also tried to solve this problem, but he has made it abundantly clear that 'with alankar' only, there is poetic-touch. We cannot separate each element and then call it style, alankar, or Kavya. It is a conglomeration of all the three. (Vakrokti Jivitam 1.6.) According to Hill also the style and thee Poetry are one and the same.

Here both - hill and Kuntak agree on the same point that the poetic language and style cannot be separated. They are inseparable. But still however, in discussion on basic principles, some consider that each is separate and stand outstanding in their own way; they brand them separately. There are as may versions as there are critics. Each one is independently separate.

In reality, Vaman has said very clearly that the poetry's hidden beauty is its embellishment/decoration and it is due to this acceptability of the ornamentation that the people accept it as acceptable - in other words Beauty + Decoration/Ornamentation = Poetry. In the same way Poetical Language + Style + Decoration = give life to the poetry. For the sake of criticism, each may be separate, but in unity, they are one and its conglomeration only makes a poetry beautiful. Just as - little Grain - large quantity of Grain/Ugly face, beautiful face/Red Flower, Green Flower/Black Hair, White Hair - in all these sentences the adjective carries different meaning, and to come at, to arrive at the meaning, we cannot separate the adjective - largeness-shortage cannot be separated from the grain, beauty and ugliness cannot be separated from the face and in the same manner, Poetic Language and the style cannot be separated from each other; In reality, they are two in one.

Now let us have a look at this with the viewpoint of Indian view- point: There are four categories reserved for this - as under:

1. Kashta Jatu Nyay,
2. Karna-Kundal Nyay,
3. Jaltarang Nyay,
4. Pat Tantu Nyay.

**Kashta Jatu Nyay** - Some trees generally ooze one sort substance called 'Gum' - it is attached to the tree, we can separate it, but cannot re-fix it.

**Karna-Kundal Nyay**. Ear rings are put on ears. When they are worn, they gave decoration to the beauty; when they are removed, its beauty is removed - this is called Karna Kundal Nyay. This is called 'Ashrya-Ashryee Sambandh' - one is attached with the other.

**Jal Tarang Nyay** - We can see the waves in the sea; sea is full of waves, but we cannot separate waves from the sea. Sea has waves. Water is full of Waves, and yet one cannot be separated from the other. One is attached to the other inseparably.

**Pat-Tantu Nyay** - The cloth is made up of yarn. The collection of yarn is cloth. When yarn is not there, the cloth is also not there. This position in sanskrit is called 'Anvay-Vyatirek- Sambandh'; Again one is dependent on another. Absence of one, is absence of other. When there is one there is another; when one is not there, the other is not there. The first is 'Anvay', the other is 'Vyatirek'.

**This very principle** - formula of four points - is applicable to the poetry also, in a very delicate manner; we shall see them one by one.

1. In the poetic language, the position of style is not equivalent to 'Kashta Jatu Nyay', because you can remove the gum from the tree separately, but in the poetic language, you cannot detach 'style' and language. Nor the style in any

way jumps out of falk- language, nor you can separate it from the Poetic language.

2. Nor is the relation of poetic language with 'Karna-Kundal Nyay', because these two factors are unseparable. One cannot make poetic language from the folk-language; nor one can separate style from poetic language and make it turn into common language.

3. Nor is the position of poetic language confined to 'Jal-Tarang- Nyay' because, the style cannot be separated from the poetic language. The question does not arise about the separation.

4. But to be precise the position of the poetic languages can easily be compared to 'Pat-tantu Nyay'. By cloth we mean the weaving of yarn, - it is a solid substance and there is hidden the dexterity of the weaver. The feeling of the poet can be described by a common man in an ordinary folk-language; the public is not aware of the fact that yarn and cloth both are not separable. The small/big sentences are moulded into poetic language and there lies the beauty of the composer, just as that of a weaver, who manufactures yarn/cloth The sentences in a poetry are the weaving of words in the poetry and the style, therefore, cannot be separated. We must state the combination of yarns as poetic language.

## Section II

We shall now discuss about the poetic language vis-a-vis the style. On account of many reasons, the ordinary language is quite a distance from Poetic Language. In ordinary language, there is some serene standard, but in poetic language it diversifies. And hence one can see this deviation from the rut - away from the local interpretation. There are many factors attached to the poetic language; but that does mean that its importance is relegated. This element is very useful. Generally the standard routine gets deviation and this change of course is designated as Poetic Language.

Language in common parlour is the synonym of poetry; Sentence means a collection of small words together. These sentences are powerful enough to express the meaning very clearly. In this very sentence, there is possibility of ambition and its use is variegated In each sentence there is some action. It may be direct/oblique; or it may not be there too. There are many words in a sentence; some times even one word makes a sentence. 'May I bring water for you' is a question mark and its reply so concisely compact that it reply in one word 'Yes' carries a large sentence - please, a glass of water for me; it should not he hot or cold; Thus both the question and its answer are important.

Having gone through this, now let us have a look from the angle of poetic Language. Is there any independent status of the sentence in context with the language - the reply is 'No'. For Example, 'He Alone' - 'He' - 'Came' these words are the subject of the Dictionary, but not that of language. 'He came' - there is a complete sentence and it becomes a subject of 'Language'. It is agreed that it is only on the language of the poetry that the criticism is undertaken - although it is a matter of stylistics'. Thus it is to be considered in context with the fore-ground/back- ground - the sentence has no independent existence; Literally one sentence is attached with joined with another sentences and the meaning would come only when entire context is taken into consideration and not by selection of separate sentences. In the previous we have seen the use of word 'Tati....' - here the reference is not related to one word only but it is related with the entire context. Thus we can conclude that the poetic language is a collection of words/sentences which exhibits their internal quality/beauty.

Let us have a look - a quick cursory look at the sayings of other people on the subject :

(a) Style, in the absolute sense, is a complete fashion of the personal and the universal. (John Milton Marry)

(b) Literary style is a means by which one personality moves others (F.L. Lucas, Style. p. 38)

(c) Style: writer's way with words, as Buffon observed, 'The style is the man himself'.
(The Reader's Digest Great Encyclopedic Dictionary. Vo. 3. p. 1060)

Now let us have a different angle to look at Poetic Language. Every writer's angle of vision is quite different from the other - it is a well known fact. His personality is categorically imprinted on his writings and it is this reason as to why - big personalities like Valmiki, Kalidas, Ashwaghosh, Bharavi, Dandi, Magh, Jaydev, all these poets writings, there is a wide and varied distance - and the this very mode, method, manner, is branded as their own peculiar 'Style'. Thus we can conclusively arrive at a statement that - 'any poet's writing-system, his method of using words, sentences, his weaving of ideas, his exhibition of thoughts, through the medium of words, language, etc. is branded as his own 'Style' - this is poetic language.

**Ambiguity**

Having elaborately dealt with the subject of 'Style', we shall now take up a new topic viz., 'Ambiguity' - what is this, let us analyse it further.

There is a special form of a poetic language. Words represent grammar, but at the level of its interpretation, it is quite different from different angles. Thus this ambiguity is a quality positive or negative - all by itself. When it is involved in the matter of ambiguity, it becomes an attraction; this is the speciality of poetic language.

Now what is ambiguity? When only one sentence gives two or more different meaning out of the same sentence, it means that the statement made is apparently ambiguous. For Example, he decided on the boat. This has two meanings - out of the surface structure, there is possibility of two hidden (deep) structure, again:

(a) He chose the boat.

(b) He decided while he was on the boat.

According to different authors :

– more than one cognitive meaning for the same piece of language. (A linguistic guide to English Poetry - Page 207)

– true ambiguity rests on a permanent failure to find a single satisfactory syntax. A single surface reflects more than one deep structure. (Stylistics p. 99)

– ambiguity is doubtful meaning of sentences sharing the same surface structure but with different structures. (Linguistics and Literature p. 113).

Ambiguity is accepted at such places, where from an outer

structure, there is possibility of more than other structures underneath. According to relevance, only one meaning or structure is desired to be applied, but for the sake of criticism, one has to find out what it actually means.

But when the ambiguity is removed, something sprouts out of it, and it becomes the reason for the beauty of the poetry. We give below an example from the poetry of 'Auden' - 'The Wanderer'

> *There head falls forward, fatigues at evening, and dreams of home,*
> *Waving from window, spread of welcome.*
> *Kissing of wife under single sheet;*
> *But waking sees*
> *Bird-flocks nameless to him, through doorway voices of new men making another love.* *(Stylistics p. 99)*

Here the word 'Dreams' leads us to the meaning of 'dream only' and then the poetry becomes ambiguous. But when we take the word 'dream' as an action of 'mind' - we turn to 'Head-Dreams', then the poetry becomes quite clear and pleasant. The traveller in the evening - tired and toiled thinks about his welcome to home, by waving hands from the window, when the wife sleeping under the cover is ready for a sweet kiss, he is dreaming (he is imagining things). But when he is awake, he looks at the collection of birds, the names of which are not known to him. He hears the voices coming from the door - they are ready to welcome him (just to make him irritate to burn his heart)

This is indeed, really marvellous; what is the original apparent meaning, and really, when explained, translated, and taught, the meaning is altogether different; pleasure turns into sorrow; expectations are turning sour and life becomes a problem - this is called 'dream' He thinks about fanciful but reality is quite different from what it is. This is ambiguity.

*Let us take an example in Marvell's lines:*

> *Meanwhile the mind from pleasure less,*
> *Withdraws into its happiness.*

should be understand that the mind is less because of pleasure of that because of less pleasure the mind withdraws ? The answer now was to be 'Both - and what else can you find ? (Stylistics P. 101)

As it is ambiguity is a 'defect'; but when one sentence is in the form of two, and if one creates ambiguity, but the second one brings clarity, the reader gets one sort of pleasure, just as a child gets after solving his mathematic problem. The poetry above gives us the same position. 'Dreams' when it becomes symbolic, till then there is some ambiguity, but when we accept it as a 'verb', the matter become quite clear. According to Indian interpretation, it is said as 'Pad Vakrata' - 'Obliqueness of sentence'. Now we shall have to elaborate this 'Pad Vakrata - meaning 'Pad Purvardh Vakrata or 'Pad Padarth Vakrata' - in all there are 19 classifications but there is no sub-classification, which can understand the practical position. We may brand this classification as 'Pad-Bhed - Vakrata' by the use of which one sentence can be translated into another sentence and the ambiguity may turn into clarity, just as 'Dream' is translated into two sections.

(1) Base pleasure - when this reaches a level of satisfaction, one feels guilty and he withdraws from the worldly pleasures and deviated towards the higher plain of metaphysics.

(2) The above is an example of an excess of basic pleasures - just opposite to it is the deficiency of experience of basic pleasures, and here also the same reaction comes into play, when one meanders towards metaphysics and weans his tendencies from the worldly pleasures towards philosophical atmosphere and environments. "Dhatushu Kshiyamaneshu Shama Kasya na jayate ? - this is an example.

Now on account of these ambiguities, the pundits of Indian poetry consider this as an ornamentation such as 'Slash', 'Virodhabhas' 'Parisamkhya', etc. and it some time it is called 'Sandigdha- Dosha' also. Here also we would like to quote a sanskrit example:

"Sakalkalam purmetatjjatam samprati sudhamshubimbamiv" Sahityadarpan 10.12. This city has been just like copy of moon. 'Sakalkala' means full of all the 'Kalas' of chandra. Here there is 'Slash' Alankar. For non-clarity 'Ashspashta Dosha' we shall have to refer to Kavya Prakash Shloka 7/154, where the word 'Vandyam' carries double meaning. - not an arrested person, but a respected person. That is why this is called 'Sandigotha dosha'.

Now take one more example - "Sa Mahatma Bhagvashnmahapadam upaatah". One meaning is that by good (luck) he got a higher position/status, but if sandhi is taken into consideration, the meaning would be quite entirely different, meaning the Mahatma met the ultimate salvation 'Abhgyavashat' - by misfortune; Now to this 'Dosha' Bhamah has called 'Kalpa-Dushta-Dosha' from his point of view.

Non-clarity has another angle also in English language also there are words which are phonetacally similar, but the meaning of each is quite different, just as 'Sore - Soar' 'Bound' 'Gilt-Guilt', etc. there are many in number but for want of space, we do not ennumerate all of them. - these are only for the sake of examples only. Here we cannot but help giving an example from Shakespeare's 'Romeo Juliat', when the dialogue is as under:

*You are a lover; borrow cupid's wings,*
*and soar with them above a common bound,*

Where Romeo replies that -

*I am too sore enpierced with his shalft,*
*to soar with his light feathers, and so bound, woe.*
*I cannot bound a pitch above dull*

*(Romeo and Juliet I, IV)*

Here the double meaning of the words creates suspense, and there is further :

*and three corrupted men*
*have, for the gilt of France - Oguilt indeed*
*confirmed conspiracy with fearful France*

*(Henry, V, II, Chorus)*

The same position is in the following piece also, where the word 'Pitch' has created marvellous effect:

*but soon he found*
*The welkin pitched with sullem clouds around,*
*An eastern wind, and dew upon the ground*

*(Dryden, Death of Amyntas)*

Here the word 'pitch' has two meanings (1) Pitching a tent and (b) making black covering with pitch' and the meaning is quite different; in the sky the clouds have pitched tent of clouds and the sky has been tarnished with black colour. Eastern wind is blowing and it sprays dew on the earth.

In the following lines, the word 'port' is significative:

*Where Bentley late tempestuous wont to sport*
*in troubled waters, but now sleeps in part.*

*(Pope, Dunciad IV)*

Port meant - (1) the sea-shore (2) a type of wine. Bentley is lying under the influence the wine Port.

Thus in Indian poetry also such sort of 'Shabda-Shlesh' is not uncommon. The word 'harbour' has a different meaning, the word 'wine' has a different meaning. Then the critics brand this as 'Ambiguity' or 'Inter-determinacy'; In sanskrit language, one would find many 'Shabda-alankars', which carry different meanings.

*'Mitratri putranetray.........*
*..........Gotratre te namo namah."*

Indian poetics brands this as picturesque-word-picture; Here the irony is suppressed and it does not come out as it should. It is true that the word-combination is so impressive that the reader is impressed at the very first reading, but when, he faces ambiguity, he becomes non-plus and he has to take the resort to the lexicon to arrive at what the writer wishes to convey.

Then we have to take into consideration the ambiguity of the words, with the ambiguity of the meaning also for example,

*"Colourless green ideas sleep furiously"*
*(Linguistics and literature p. 1)*

Apparently the words are aligned alright, but the real meaning there of causing confusion, makes the reader's mind wander, as to what does the writer wishes to convey to the reader by this version. Thus ambiguous interpretation creates confusion, and we shall have to be bold enough to accept 'fault' as fault only!

According to Indian poetics, if the current meaning is not forthcoming and a different meaning is intended by the writer, it is called 'Irony', but then it leads to ambiguity also. e.g.

*"Ravina Hrutsaubhagyatusharavruta mandalah:*
*............(Sahitya Darpan 4.3)*

Here the Moon has been branded as 'Blind', where as it has

been used for the reader, who has lost the power of sight to see, here they have called the 'mirror' as 'Blind' on account of the fact that the mirror has lost the power to reflect on account of dew covered on the mirror. With reference the 'moon' reflects 'good fortune' and not the light. Here the word 'Blind' is misguiding - this is one sort of ambiguity. According to Indian poetic this type of poetry is addressed as 'Atyant-Tiraskrut-Vachya-Dhwani- Kavya".

Now we shall give you one more example, where the ambiguity is not on account of one word or one sentence, but on account of the entire couplet, which has two meanings -

*"Gachha Gachhasi chet kant panthanah santu te Shivah'*

Here the meaning is this that according to 'Nayika', if Nayak goes away, Nayika may die and that is why it is conveyed that the Nayak should not go. This brand is branded as 'Vastu-Dhwani- Kavya'.

Now still one more example to stress the argument about non-clarity - mis-giving :

*"Raghav virah jwala santapitsahya Shail Shikhereshu'*

*(Rasagangadhara 1)*

Having had the separation of Sita, Rama's fire of separation, agony of separation was so hot that the Sahya mountain picks were also hot, where Vanar-sena was residing - now these monkeys began to be angry with Hanuman in this regard. Then thus the question arises, why the vanar group should get angry with Hanuman. Because Hanuman did not inform Shree Rama about the Sita's whereabouts and welfare; When Shree Ram heard the news, his separation fire began to cool down and the Hill-picks too began to cool down simultaneously. This prose clarification is not there in the poetical version and that is by the quality of non- clarity, this poetry is branded as 'Asphut-Gunibhut-Vyanga- Kavya'.

In fine, we give here one more example to stress and impress what has been said here to fore. There are many examples of non-clarity, and it is cleared subsequently, and it gives out poetical embellishment. But over and above this, there are some non-clear usage of words are also taken into consideration, when one word has several meanings and one has to find out which meaning is at and appropriate according to the text and context of the prose of poetical order. There are 14 such usages in the Indian Poetics, which are used 'Vishesh-

Smruti-Hetu' 'For the sake of special remembrance', through the help of which the correct meaning is arrived at. In Sanskrit they are ennumerated as : 'Samyog', 'Viprayog', 'Sahcharya', 'Virodhita', Artha- Pryojana', 'Prakarana', 'Ling', 'Symbol', 'nearness of other word' 'Samarthya', 'Auchiti', - 'fitness', 'Desh', 'Kala', 'Vyakti', 'Swar', etc. To corroborate, we give below few examples :

– Sthanum Bhaja Bhavachhide - 'To cross this samsara, pray 'Sthanu'

– Here 'sthanu' has many meaning, which are not to be taken into consideration - here it applies to only Lord God Shiva - meaning if one wishes to cross this Bhavsager, he should resort to Lord God Shiva only. (Meaning -Reason)

– Kupito Makardhawajah - the 2nd word has also many meanings and here it touches only 'cupid', because anger has much to do with 'Cupid' (Ling - Chinha - Symbol)

– Madhuna Matta Kokila' - Here Madhu has many meaning, but here the correct interpretation relate to season 'Spring' only. (Capacity)

– Chitrabhanu Bhati Nishayam - Chitrabhanu is Sun, but here in the night, it relates to 'fire' only and that is why (TIME) is the correct solution.

Thus we conclude that a word having many meaning conveys the correct meaning only when correct interpretation is arrived at. Thus 'Non-Clarity' also has its important role in the poetic literature in the whole and in general - it plays a very important role in its own way, creating miracle - Chamatkar in all the ways. Correct interpretation stuns the reader; he is be- spelled; be-wildered, he is flabbergasted - dumb founded, astonished. One of the important topic of the linguistic - stylistics is **Irrationality and Paradox** which we are going to discuss here :

In the Poetic literature one of the forms of the poetry is according to grammatical rules, and as far as arrangements of words are concerned - they appear to be normal, but at the level of the meaning thereof, there appears a slight variation which creates irrationality and/or Paradox - both. But this could be accepted only when some miracle is created out of it, as is in the case of non-clarity.

This sort of Irrational or Paradoxical are so framed and incorporated among the main stream that it tuns out to be miraculous and these are generally found in religious books or in the discourse of religious heads. e.g.

*I die, yet depart not,*
*I am bound, yet soar free;*
*Thou are and thou are not*
*And ever Shalt be!*

*(Robern Buchanan; the city of Dreams)*

Having read this, we also come across Shanti-path lines of "Ishavasyopanishad", which are quited below :

*"Purnamadah Purnamidam Purnat Purnamudchayate......*
*Puranasya Purnamaday Purnamevavshishyate -*

*(Ishopanishad).*

meaning - this is complete, that is complete, complete is taken out of complete, and then complete only remains, when complete is taken out of complete.

We may have to elaborate this further -

This Brahma is complete. This world is also complete. If un-seen Brahma is taken out of this seeming world, which can come out of it only - the seeming world has come out of unseeming Brahma only - only the Brahma remains, when the world is taken out of Brahma. By uttering this paradoxical statement, we praise the magnitude of the divine power. That is what creates Irrationality and paradoxical situation. We, the mundane worldly people, how can we arrive at the vastness/immenseness of the incomprehensible, ununderstandable, unapproachable, indecipherable 'Brahma'. Again there is an English thought :

*But he that hides a dark soul and foul thoughts,*
*Benighted walks under the midday sun.*

*(Milton, Comus.)*

The day light of the noon and still darkness ! How much paradoxical statement it is. If a sinful man is shown in day light, even then his fall is eminent and that is why such places and such contexts are inter-woven at various places, in the poetical realm, and that is why 'Irrationalism in Poetry or 'Paradox' in poetry is always in lime light.

And yet another poet Dance comes out with a very peculiar verse in his poetry - 'The Legacy': wherein by using the pronoun, 'I', he has created a miraculous situation :

*"Though I be dead, which sent me, I should be*
*mine own executor and legacy."*

*(Stylistics p. 191)*

The meaning of this is abundantly clear - Even if I die, I have sent me, and I am my Killer; whatever legacy I leave behind, is mine.

About one "Donne" it is written that 'He was a master of the poetic use of pronouns ..... and he explored the possibilities of the pronoun with an ingenuity that remains surprising. The Book, "The Legacy" contains this couplet - 'Though I be dead .....' Stylistics. p. 191).

But before these two lines, there is one more line -

*'I die as often as from the I go,.....'*

meaning, as many times I be away from you, every time I die - even though I appear to be living - without you I am dead. Meaning, I am 'a lover' and you - God - 'Beloved = both are one. Separate existence is just impossible. When it is elaborately explained, we arrive at some confounding conclusion, but even then suggestion is not clear; Can the meaning be arrived at as under: 'Even if I die, you have sent me away and I have sent myself to you. You are my killer and this my property will be left to you.'

The poet Dome's this poetry has been used by Turner because, the pronoun 'i' has been poetically used. Although this poetry has been or can be branded as 'Klisht-kavya' 'difficult poetry', because in this poetry (according to Kit-Bhrungi Nyay) lover ad beloved both are used in pronoun 'I' in the third person or sometime in second person - that also at random, not according to any rules. Even after so much discussion, the meaning is not completely clear.

According to Indian Poetics, this can be used as 'direct' poetry - Lakshana Shabda Shakti' - where the letter 'I' has been used for 'the reader' and when 'Thou' is used it is also in the same sense and even then it has been branded with 'Lisht Dosha'. Turner wishes to show us the magic of the use of letter 'I'. Here in Indian poetics, Kuntak has branded it as 'Pad Padardh Vakrata' and under it has been shown as in 'first', 'second' and 'third' person.

Here we would like to elaborate upon 'Kit Bhringi Nyay'. When an insect is dead, and when butter-fly or the Bee, flies over the Insect, it becomes Bee and the poet has used this tac-tic to express himself effectively.

Further we may take liberty to quote Kumar Sambhav, 5/40

"*Atotra kinchid bhavatim Bahukshamam.........*
*..........na ched rahasyam praktivatumarhati.*"

In the disguised-dress of a Brahmachari, Mahadevji says to Parvati - 'He Tapodhane, Parvati - this Brahman (Meaning Mahadevji himself) being an obstinate person, asks of you, a beautiful lady, please do not take it ill; if it is not secret, kindly reply.

Here also Mahadevji instead of useing himself as 'first person', he expresses himself in 'third person', which inculcates poetic miracle and similarly Donne's sentence 'though I be dead....' is not as clear as Sanskrit quoted above, but then we have to accept 'Purush-Vakrata' - meaning the poet has used his dexterity to let out two meanings out of the use of one word only - that is what the poet aims at. In such 'high-tone poetry', the difference between 'I' and 'You' comes to an end just as 'Aham Brahmasmi' - 'Tat twam asi'. The more difficult the composition is, more it is acceptable at large.

Here we shall discuss a different point. There is a rare figure of speech called 'Hendiadys' (Greek for 'One thing by means of two'), the expression by means of co-ordinate groups of what is properly expressed in a single group. Frances Thompson's 'And with the sea-breeze - 'will illustrate this. 'She' and 'innocence' are not in reality separate, but are separated by linguistic device. (Stylistics p. 197).

This irrationality has been shown interestingly by Turner in his couplet resorting to 'Hendiadys' mentioned above. For example take this Francis Thompson's couplet:

"*And with the sea-breeze hand-in-hand,*
*came innocence and she.*'

*(Stylistics B. 108)*

Here the 'Innocence' and 'she' are not two separate entity; this dame is so 'fault-less' that the poet does not want to convey 'She is innocent', but poetically he has used the words in such a way as to appear two separate identity, and this usage has been an embellishment of the poetic art. In Indian poetry also there may be examples, where, adjective has been used as a symbolic item, and Innocence has been made to walk with a person; this may be branded as 'Poetic liberty' to have used adjective in altogether a different live form - as if walking hand in hand with the person. It is a superb art of expression.

Sometimes such sort of usage leaves a bad taste in the mouth, for example, just have this piece:

*I dislike giggling school girls, don't you ?*
*I don't know, I've never giggled one.*

(*Stylistics p. 109*)

The meaning is clear that the writer does not approve the manner in which school girls laugh bluntly; because the writer has not liked that in the past (It has other meaning also, which is not written here). By going through this pleasureful answers, we come across "Vakrokti"'s sub-division called 'Slash-Vakrokti'. In Sanskrit there are many such incidents/quotations and here is a one for an example-

"*Kim Gauri Mam prati Rusha ? Nanu Gauraham Kinm Kupyami Kam Prati?*

(*Rudrat - Kavyalankar 2.15*)

Mahadevji asks Parvati ji - "Oh Gauri, Why are you angry with me ? Parvati intentionally translated this sentence with breaks in a different way - 'Oh Cow why you are displeased with me ? and then definitely Parvatiji asks of question - am I a cow ? On whom I am displeased ? In this way in the whole Shloka, there is a nice discussion between the two -lover and beloved -

Thus thee usage of opposite words and to create an effect of magic is not new for linguistics - in any language you will come across such a manipulation, e.g., Lat us take Shakespeare's Romeo and Juliet, and then the Juliet at the time of departure says that

*'Parting is such a sweet sorrow!'*

(*Romeo & juliet - 11.11.*)

To describe separation as sweet pain is also abundantly quoted in Indian Poetics - it is a special formation of decoration, e.g.

*'Tav Virahe Malay Marut dwanalah .............*

*(Sahitya Darpana 10.68.)*

'In your absence even the pleasing Malay wind is just like a fire, Moon-beam-rays are hot, and pains the heart and lotus leaf has become hot sun.'

Then there is 'Vasham Alankar', - thus -

*"Anandmamidam Kuvalayadallochane dadasi twam,.....*

*(Sahitya Darpana 10.70)*

Oh lotus eyed lady, you give me immense pleasure, but the separation created by you, gives me immense dis-pleasure.' In Hindi literature also, we come across such sort of 'Non-Clarity' (Aspashtata) Non-relevance' (un-relatedness) 'Opposition' (Virodh) at many places and it is settled through the medium of 'direct meaning' Lakshna' only. The few examples from Kamayani:

- *Pawan pi raha the shabdokon....Chinta. 70*
- *Usha sunahare tir barasati ......Asha 1.*
- *Madhumay vasant jivan van ke,...... Kam 1.*
- *Mai jabhi tolane ka karti....... Lajja 42.*
- *Anchal latakati nishitani......Karma 46.*

In 'New Poetry', you will find many such examples standing besides you with open mouth and the problems are solved too easily, but even then there are some quotations which still remain unsolved - un-understood inspite best efforts. 'Japani Lalten si Khub-surat....Nitesheke Dari-Keshavchad Varma.

- *Shakho per jame dhup ke fahe.... Kedarnath Sinh.*
- *Mai Vanshi-Man hamari du dh ka tary. Thakurprasad Sinh*

*in English:*

- *Thou are to me a delicious torment.*
- *To live a life half-dead, a living death.*
- *And love's the noblest frailty of the mind.*

In all these saying there is opposite effect:

(a) Tum mere liye madhur Yantrana ho -

(b) Jite je mar jana

(c) Prem to manke prashastam durbalta hai.

Take an example from Abhignan Shakuntala by Kalidas, where Dushyant complaints that the rays of the moon sprays hot heat and the Cupid while sending flower arrows hits hard.

*"Tav Kusum Sharatwam, Shit Rashmitvamindo,*

*(Abhignan. 33)*

In this way in may places such contradictory statements are used profusely. This is due to manipulations of the usage of conflicting words:

*'Yasya Vrana tasyaev Vedana Bhanati Natijjanalikam.*

*(Kavya Prakash 10.534)*

Meaning the one who is injured- he is the one who suffers people say such like things, but that is not true. Inasmuch, when husband puts marks of 'Dant-Nakha-Kshata' on the wife, these would becomes the reason for jealosusy for other."

This is 'Asangati Alankar', but the it is believed to be a miracle - and it is accepted as such.

In this way, Irrationality and paradox, both some times alone and sometimes together, sometimes in short form some times in a wide vista-vision, creates miracles in the poetic field and all these - opposition - difference - obtuse-oblique-interpretation, irrelevance - all these normally not accepted in their proper meaning, but in the poetical atmosphere, when they carry quite the opposite meaning, they do not hurt, but become an embellishment, an ornament, a delicacy for the reader, for the critic and the rest.

**Difference in Linguistic Structure**

The term 'style' is not easy to define precisely. Roughly speaking two utterances in the same language, which convey approximately the same information, but which are different in their linguistic structure, can be said to differ in style. Stylistic variations within a single language are universal, and in many cases, there are certain special styles which are felt to be peculiarly appropriate to certain circumstances.

*(A course in Modern Linguistics. p. 556)*

When Haquet says the above statement, it is clear that according to the circumstances and situation, different style is undertaken on an experimental basis. And this very varied manifestation is branded as 'Difference in Linguistic structure'. To confirm this, we give the following examples from the Indian Poetry by Kavyacharya Shree Vaman: - What the poet says is this that when wind waves the twig, or the creeper, the bee to dances with the movement; the poet puts this very version in the following lines:

A. Vilulit Makaranda Manjarirnartayanti.

B. Vilulit Madhudhara Manjari lolayanti.

*(Ka.Su.Vru. 3.1.5)*

According to Vaman, in the first line there is 'Oaja' 'Ghadbandhatvam Oajah', but in the second sentence there is not Gadhatva but Shithilatva. In both 'Vilulit' and 'Manjarir' both the words are alike, but the difference is in other words - In one there is 'Makaranda' and 'Nartayanti', whereas in another where as in the other, there is 'Madhudhara' and 'Lolayanti'. Due to first there is Gadhatva, due to the second there is 'Shithilatva'. Vaman has not thrown light on this, as to why and how this two are branded as such separately, but his critic Gopendratripurhar Bhuapal has thrown light on this. In the first Makaranda', 'Nda' is a joint letter; and in 'Narta yanti' also there is 'R' dancing and there is 'Gadhatva' in this and in the absence of this in the second, the position is quite different, and as such is 'shithilatva' - the absence of 'Oaja'.

The poet wants to manifest that the anklets of the dancers makes tinkling noise and on the very basis, the following two lines will make you feel a feeling of dancing and Vaman brands this quality as 'Udarata'; Whereas in the second version, the situation is quite different;

A. Swacharanavinivishtai Nupurainartakinam,
Zaniti Ranitamasitatatra chirra kalancha.

B. Charankamallagni Nupurai Nartakinam,
zatiti ranitmasinmanju Chitrancha tatra.

*(Ka.Su.Vru. 3.1.23)*

Haket is right when he says that according to the situation, the style takes a turn and that is why he wants to manifest two different examples where two different Styles are included.

In the drama called 'Priyadarshika', the king is afraid of angry 'Vasavadatta', and on the second side, having seen 'Aranyaka', he is attracted towards her beautiful face, and under these circumstance the poet has four lines, in the first two lines, he has used one style, and in another two another style.

The first two lines involve 'Kathor Shaili' (Godi Riti), where as the second two lines invoke 'Komal Shaili' (Vaidarbhi Riti)

> *"Swedambhah manabhinnabhishamatar Bhrubhangamekem rusha*
>
> *Trasenapermutplutototpluta mrugvyalola netrotpalam-*
>
> *'Utpashyanahmagrato mukhmidam devya priyayanstatha,*
> *Bhitschotsukamansascha mahati Kshiptosmyamaham Sankate."*

*(Priyadarshika)*

On one side, I see the lotus eyes of Vasavdatta. Due to anger her eye-brows have given way to sweat-water and thus they have become dangerous and now her eyes are so shown that due to anger, they are dancing as if deers which are very active. But then simultaneously he looks at the face of 'Aaranyika' - now on one side he looks at the angry face of 'Vasavadatta' and on the other side, having a look at 'Aranyika', he is in dilema."

If you are interested, have a look at another poem, where they are praying 'Nrusinha', and simultaneously expects his blessings. The Prayog is that of 'Gadhbandha', but step by step, this goes down, as

> *"Projjwalujjawal...........*
>
> *Patu vo Narkesari."*

*(Sa.Da. 7.8.)*

The rule is that the style should be maintained through out. What is in the beginning, must be at the end also. This quality, according to 'Vamana' is 'Samata'. Margabhedah Samata' (Ka.Su.Vru. 3.1.12), but here, Gadhbandha has not been maintained from 1st to last, and hence there is 'Patat-Prakasrhata-Dosha' in this shloka, but yet there is no 'Dosha' here, because in the 4th Charana they expect blessings in the 'Komal Bandha'.

Linguistic structure is definitely a complicated subject, if we go into detail. For example in Sanskrit, the word 'Tata' is used in all the three genders - Masculine, feminine, and neuter gender - Tatah, tati, Tatam, and in common parlour or in poetical expression, it can be used according to context. In the following shloka, the word 'Tati' is used knowingly so that it expresses the feeling of the 'Nayika', taking into consideration that the 'Nayak' - the Megha' will quench her thirst:

"*Tati taram Tamyatyatishashiyashah kaupi Jaladah:*
*................................Bhuvanvalayakrantsubhagah:*

*(V.Ji.2/79).*

Let us discuss the subject further. In general parlour, the speaker used his own views to express what he wishes to convey, but when he can't use specialised language, it is inability to do so. But in poetical language, one has to be very wary about composition of the poetry. In the Indian poetic field, Kavyacharya Anandvardhan has branded this as 'Sanghatana', which according to stylistics is named as 'Samrachana', meaning construction of sentences. For this purpose, the following four points must be born in mind: 1. The speaker. 2. The speech, 3. The subject. and the 4th one 'Rasa' - the suggestion/interest. According to Valendar, also, he has stated four main points in this regard. Viz. The characters of the subject (2) The aim thereof (3) readers' status and the (4) the position/status of the writer.

Style in the linguistic sense usually signifies every special usage clearly contrasted against the general. More clearly, style could be defined as that way of presenting a subject which differ more or less from the average and which is motivated by the character of the subject the purpose of the presentation, the reader's qualification and the writer's personality.

*(An approach to the Style; Linguistics & Style)*

Clearly the Indian Poet Anandvardhan and the Western writer Valendar both deal with the same subject matter. According to Indian Standard, we can discuss in detail as under:

1. Vakroauchitya - Either the poet or any poet-formed character is there. The character is Hero or some one else. There are four types of Heroes - Dhirodatta, Dhirodhdhatta, Dhiralalit, and Dhirprashanta. The poet always uses the interesting language with sentimental touch but then sometimes he has to express himself without the help of either. According to the fitness of the characters, Assessments, Alpasamasa, or Dirgha samasa fitness are creating magic at every stage.
2. Appropriateness of Language. This refers to the subject to be described or the story. They are of two types - they can be or cannot be staged and they are also related to first, second or third rate standards. The characterization would be according to plot or story.
3. Appropriateness of the subject. Vishayauchitya- This depends upon the form of the poetry - it may be descriptive, or in couplets, prose + poetry, a poetical scene, a story - long or short - etc. Everything is to be born in mind. For example in Epic or Lyric, even if the story is quite perfect, we have to be careful. In drama in scenes relating to 'Raudra Rasa', there should not be use of 'Dirgha Samasa.'

It has been mentioned in 'Kavyanushashan, 4th Canto - that in the Akhyayika, there should be continuity, but in Shringar Rasa, only delicate words are to be used and not harsh. In 'Katha' there should be lucidity - may the description be that of 'Raudra Rasa'. Because the reader of 'Akhyayika' is of a special dass. where as the reader of 'Katha' is a common man. The same relates to dramas also the observers of dramas come from common level but the opinion differs.

4. Rasauchitya - Appropriateness of 'Rasa' - The story should be according to Rasa. There should be a balanced composition in different 'Rasas'. In sorrowful circumstances, separation, Shrungar or in 'Shanta rasa', there should be delicate use of words whereas in the 'Rasas' having 'Vir', Raudra', 'Bhayanak, the construction should be altogether different.

Anandvardhan is of the opinion that the all the four points

mentioned above, viz., Vakta, Vachya, Vishay and Rasa, they have no individual identity, but its compact formation is advisable for construction. The separation has been shown only for the sake of explaining the details. We have therefore to be vigilent when we arrive at a conclusion that what Anandvardhan has said above is quite justified. Any item taken single - independently - it would not carry any meaning; because these are complementary, one is related to, attached to another and as such a combination of all the four only would bring a desired result - desired effect - the impact - on the mind of the reader - observer - listener.

First of all let us take 'Rasa' - The Nayak, who is Dhiralalit, while discussing 'Love' with his beloved, would discuss his love affairs in quite a different language, other than, when one fighter in his war time battle field challenges the other fighter in a very very harsh, tone, voice and vociferous words. When Udayan talks to Vasavadatta, his tone and approach is too delicate because it is full of 'Shringara Rasa', - but when Bhimsen talks to his enemies in the battle field, his speech in terrific, terrible and tumultous. The language of both the people, according to the circumstances of each case very a lot. Udayan speech would be quite delicate and the speech by Duryodhan or Bhima would be long winding sentences and samasas. Vasavadatta uses language which is soft and delicate - the letters would be themselves soft whereas in other case the letters too would be harsh. Thus in some 'Rasa' the letters are delicate whereas in others they are harsh, according to circumstances and characters. For example in Uttar Ramcharita, When Ram explains to Sita, about the situation prevalent at the time of their vanavasa, he narrates in shloka as under 'Alas Lalit Mugdha....Yatra Nidramavapta.' U.R.Ca. 1/24. In Shrungara Rasa, at other place, a separated person (Virahi), expresses his anger towards 'Kamdeva', - at this place - some use of harsh words becomes 'Guna' on account of appropriate situation. Kavya Prakash - 8/34 Sahitya Darpana 8.3-4, Kavya Prakash 8/75, Sahitya Darpana 8.5-7, there is a clear description about using delicate letters which are indicative of 'Madhurya Guna' - there are no Samasas.

Leech Suggests:

(i) that as voiced consonants have a more relaxed articulation than their voiceless counter parts, the presence of voice suggests softness, and

(ii) that consonants can be graded from the point of their hardness; fricative and aspirates being harder than liquids and nasals, affricates being harder than fricatives and aspirates, and plosives being the hardest of all.

(The nature and scope of Stylistic. p. 62)

Moreover- 'Vaktari Krodhasamyukte....
Dushravatvan Guno Bhavet (Sa.Da.7/16).

Tadivichhedkrushasya.........
....Punarasavastam Samastatmana. (Sa.Da.7.16).

In Uttar Ram Charita Natak - The Vidyadhar Couple, when they see the efficiency of 'Lava and Kusha', expresses themselves in appropriate tone and touch:

*"Zananzani takakkanakvani kinkinnkam Dhanu....*
*Vichitramabhivartate Bhuvan Bhima Ayodhanam.....(U,R.Ch. 6.1)*

This looks good from Vidyadhara, but Sita cannot speak in such harsh - Kathor - Language, although in the first act on page 15, very Sita uses long drawn sentences - just for a change.

**Story**

Now we talk about the Story. According to Indian Kavya shashtra, the story has to be seen with the angle of dramatics - The hero and his acting. In descriptive language, the language will be simple - without samas or with alpa-samas. Because the public, which hears this contains all sort of people - educated and otherwise;

But in Epics, the hearers are from upper class and are already educated, and that is why the language of such long poetry are always sophisticated. Prose order is divided into two sections - narrative and poetical; and such narrative should be strong enough to attract the attention of the public and it should be seen that in such compositions, at the time of 'Shringar' or 'Karuna Rasa', the sentences should be 'Samas-less'. The readers of the long poetry are from special class and hence its construction also should be special.

And it is due to this that the Indian Poetics is divided into two groups - the variety of the poetry and the reader's qualification.

At this time it is also necessary to throw some light on the personality of the writer also. His impression is always on his style and construction. In Indian Poetry, we talk about the capability of the poet which gives rise to various qualities of styles and methods. According to Kuntak, each poet has its own speciality and as such, there are as many styles and methods as many as there are poets. But even then, it can be divided into three sections; Sukumar, Vichitra, and Madhyam.

According to Kuntak, this division is varily based on psycho-analysis. The capable man and his capacity cannot be separated - they are one; here capacity means capacity to write a poem and the other is his own individuality. Here the question is so delicate that the Kuntak himself has agreed about its complicatedness.

Here a doubt arises about the creation. Capacity is internal, but learning is an out-side item, and as such individual internal quality and the obtained education two are quite separate identities and only one item cannot make a poet stand on his own legs independently - one is dependent on the other. Thus, if one is there - the capacity is there, but the knowledge and education is not here, the matter would be complicated. In the formation of a poetry, existence of both are essential.

Kuntak has solved this problem; he admits that always, there is difference based on education and knowledge. More versatile a man is, more sophisticated the version would be there due to the available knowledge. He further manifests that to obtain knowledge and education, the individual attitude of the poet must be there. If there is inclination then only, the creation of a poetry is possible.

Thus according to Kuntak, the nature of the poet is also a principle factor in creation of a poetry. This is very clear from the writings of different poets such as, Bhasa, kalidasa, Bhavabhuti, Bharavi, Dandi, Subandhu, Bhanbhatt, Magh, Jaydev, etc. All these poets have shown their own individuality speciality in their creations - one differs from the other in the matter, style and formation, creation, arrangements, ideas, thoughts, plots, and placement. Everyone has one's own angle of looking at things and this helps one a lot to form one's own imagination and picture. The poet's individuality play an important part in all the creations. One has got to differ from the other; One's individuality is a speciality.

**Structural Economy**

Poetics has its own speciality; when brevity is used, it gives a different touch to the poetry - brevity itself expresses much then expansion or aggrandisement. There are however two forms of expression - one in the style of 'Shri Ved Vyasa' - where the narration is unlimited - as vast and as lengthy as is possible, where as the other one is 'Sutratmak' - in a short pithy sentence, much is said in an extract form. 'Pitrudevo Bhava - Matrudevo Bhava - Acharya Devo Bhava - On this one pithy sentence, a lecturer can deliver lectures not only in one hour, one week, one month, but for years and hence this brevity too has its own beauty in a different form altogether.

For example we refer to the drama of Shakespeare - The Tempest - wherein at one place, pronoun is placed in a quite different manner. Prospero explains to his small child, how the persons deployed by his own brother had driven out the 'baby' - crying and shouting in the darkness of the night, out of the town·

*"....in the dead of darkness*
*The ministers for the purpose hurried thence*
*Me and thy crying self....."*

*(The Tempest I. II. 132)*

Here 'Thy' refers young child 'Miranda' and the description should have been ordinarily - 'she was crying on and on continously..." but reference is shortened by saying 'crying self'. This is the beauty of the brevity and it is appreciated in the poetics.

Another example runs like this -

*'Our hells of fire and dust outrange the innocence of air.'*

*(John Kirkpup: No Men are Foreign)*

Meaning the dust the smoke coming out of the mouth of the guns, and on account of the explosion of other detonators, and the dustful clouds created thereby creates a scene of hell before our eyes, and spoils the atmosphere and the environment.

Now have a one more taste from the book - 'Ulisysis'

*"Same blue serge dress she had two yeas age, the nap bleaching. Seen its best days. Wispish hair over her ears. And that dowdy toque, three old grapes to take the harm out of it. Shabby genteel. She used to be a tasty dresser. Lines round her mouth.*

*(James Joyce ; Ulysses')*

This prose-piece itself is self-explanatory; how shortly it has been explained, without the use of verb at each place.

Similarly to-day many new forms of experiments are made and few interesting ones are re-produced below, which are as an example of 'terse-ness and brevity':

(i) 'Many moons ago.

(ii) a few cigarettes ago

(iii) Two wives ago

*(A Linguistic Guide to English Poetry. P. 31)*

In sanskrit also such sentences are used just as - Jivem Sharadh Shatam (Let us live for 100 Monsoons) Here the season Monsoon has been used for years. Monsoon season is alright, but to use 'Moon' in the place of 'fifteen days' is rather unusual. But then there are other such usages as '....Go bhihi Shrinit Matsaram,' and 'anshu Duhanto Adhyasate Gavi'. In the first sentence the letter 'Go' relates to 'Milk' and in the second it serves the purpose of 'Leather'.

Indian poetics accepts this sort of interpretation as 'Arthntar - Sankramit-vachya-dhwani' and/or 'Atyant tiraskrut Vachya Dhwani' or 'upadanlakshana Shabda shakti'. Because when the speaker refers to 'Moon' - he does not exactly refer to the moon but to the 'Moon-Month', and as such when the words such as Cigarettes, Over-coats, or Wives are used, they refer to the 'time-element' and to threat particular object. Take one more example in this regard:-

*"The Widow-making unchilding unfathering deeps"*

*(Hopkin's the Wreck of the Deutschland)*

Here the use of word 'widow-making' has been used as 'Music-loving', 'Prize-winning' and such like sentences. 'Unfathering' and 'Unchilding' these words carry the negative 'Un', which is just like used in the play 'Lady Macheth' - the word 'Unsex' is used. Thus the usage covers a vast areana. There are many such examples in Sanskrit literature. (A linguistic guide to English Poetry - P. 31 and P. 43_. For example, we give below the four principles in this regard: 1. Luptopama, 2. Shlist Parmparik Rupak, 3. Parisamkhya Alankar and 4. Arthagat Ouj Guna':

*1. Smar Shar Visarachitaantara Mrugnayana Harate Muner-manah.* *(Kavya Prakash 10.410)*

The lady who is loaded with the arrows of the cupid, and who is having eyes like a dear tries to attract the mind of the sage. 'Here the use of word 'Mrugnayana' means, the lady's eyes are so volatile, so moving as the eyes of a dear. Here all the four elements have been used 1. One what is compared with, 2. volatile tendency - a common quality 3 and third 'just as' 'va' or 'eva'. Because upama-vachak-pad is not there, it is called 'Luptopama. In stylistics, this is considered as brevity - concise expression of a thought.

*(2) Stuyate Deva ! Sadvamshmukta ratnam na kairbhavan ?*

*(Kavya Prakash 10. 428).*

O: King You are a gem from the best family; Who does not praise you? Here the expression has a double meaning - it is on the basis of 'Vamsha' that the king has been addressed as best jewel-a pearl - because pearl comes fromthe 'Bans' - a bamboo tree. This comes under Litotes and hence it can also be called as 'tersenssfull construction' 3. Parisamkhya Alankar. There are 4 divisions, where 'negative aspeact' is in abeyance. E.G.

*'Kautilyam Kachnichaye, Karcharanadhar deleshu Regaste,*
*Kathinyam Kuch yugale, Taralatvam Nayanyorvasati.'*

*(Kavya Prakash 10.524).*

O Darling, twist is in your hair, red-ness in your hand and feet, Thickness in your breasts and restlessness in your eyes. Meaning your hair are twisted and not your heart, redness is in hand & feet and not with anyone else; restlessness is in the eyes and not in mind. All these negative aspects are un-mentioned and that is why the description comes under 'terseness' 'brevity'. According to Vaman there are 6 divisions with 2 sub-divisions :

1. Vakyarth Padbheda,
2. Vakyarth-Samas.

**A. Vakyarth-Padabheda** - Just as 'Divyeyem na bhavati kintu manushi' in this sentence the verb 'nimishati' is abstract and hence - this girl is not from heaven, but from this world, because she winks. And in another one, when the husband returns from some one else's house, the original Nayika is called 'Khandita' and this is used by Kalidas in Meghadut 39 - as under:

*'Tasmin Kale nayan salilam yoshitam khanditanam,*

*Shanti Neye Pranayabhirato Vartma Bhanostajatyashu.*

Megha is advised to leave the path of Sun, because he has just returned from some another woman to his home, and he must be wiping out tears of Khandita Nayika at that time.

Here the explanation would be necessary 'Arthasya Praudhine Aujah'

*'Padarthe Vakyavachanam, Vakyarthe cha Padabhidha,*
*Parudhivyassamasau cha Sabhipratvamevacha.*

*(Ka. Su. Vru. 3.2.2.)*

*Still another explanation :*
*'Anyopabhogchinhit Prataragachhati patir yasya sa Khandita-'*

*(Rasmanjari - 44).*

In this very context, one more word could be added and that is 'Varvarnini'.

Grishme Shita, Shite Ushna, proktasa Varvarnini.

Whose body temperature is according to climate - in hot season, she is cool, where as in cold season her body temperature is hot, and that is why she has been branded as Varvarnini - the best. Thus the words 'Nimishati', 'Khandita' and 'Varvarnini' - they carry the brand name as 'constructive brevity'.

**B. Vakyarth-Samas:** To use only one sentence, in place of a many sentences. E.G. 1. The sage is worshiping, 2. Ved is being understood from his mouth, 3. He applied his mind in Vasudeva, 4. and then he got Moksha.

*'Tapasyato Muner Vakrat, Vedarth abhigatya cha,*
*Vasudeva nivishtatma Vivesh sah param padam.'*

The poet has combined all the above-mentioned four points in one place only and according to Stylistic science, this is also, undoubtedly a case of "Constructional brevity", which is accepted by all, who know the science.

It will not be out of place, to quote one more Shloka in support of a woman who is "Varvanini". e.g.

*Shite Sukhoshna servangi, Grishme cha sukha shitala,*
*Bhartubhakta cha ya nari, vignegya varvarnini."*

*"Vadanam Varninyaha tasya satyam sudhakarh,*
*Sudhakarh kwa nu punah kalanka-vikalo bhavet.*
*"Swarga praptirananaiv dehen varvarnini,*
*Asya adhar raso Nyak Karoti itaram sudham.'*

To amplify the word, varvarnini, above quaotations have been necessary to support the view of the poet. These shlokas give such a beautiful description that it beggars description. The best woman-varvarnini."

**Onomatopoeia, Rhythm, Pause and Rhyme**

Poets have made use of appropriate sounds to reinforce the meaning of verse. Goldsmith echoes sense with sound in 'the varnish'd clock that clicked behind the door', as Auden does, in the rhythm as well as the sounds of 'the clock on the wall gives and electric tick.'

*(Stylistics, p. 64)*

**1. Use of Meaningful Sound**

The poets, in order to emphasise what he wants to convey, uses words which would give sound about what he says: there is a drum- noise; a cadence - voice that rings in the air. For examples, (a) The varnish'd clock that clock'd behind the door (Goldsmith) (b) The clock on the wall, gives an electric tick (Auden) According to turner, (a) in the first place the words 'clock' and 'click' give a soundful meaning and in second (b) the words 'electric' and 'tick' creates an atmosphere of a different type, which taken simultaneously - The clock/on the wall/gives an electric tick in this rhyme, the meaningful tune swings in the mind of the reader.

*"Ete te Kuhereshu.........*
*................gabhr payasah punya sarit sangma."*

*U.Ra.Ch. 2/30.*

In this poetry, the use of the words, 'Gad, Nad, Nadd, Goda, all these sound create a scene of a river itself and in other words Sankul, Chalat, Kallol, Kolahal, Uttal - all these creates a noise with letter '1' - a series of waves, which dash against each other, and play with the Bank of the river; the rhythm creates a play.

**2. Speed (Tune)**

Now let us discuss speed - tune. Indian poets have shown that in the quality of words 'Samadhi' and 'Udarata' are two rhyming tunes, which rise and fall with the reading or the poetry e.g. 'Niranandah Kaunde madhuni paribhuktojhitrase. 'Here there is 'rise and fall' where as in -

'Nara Shilbhrashta Vyasan eva Majjanti Taravah." 'Udarata' quality can be called where and when the words begin to dance, for example -

*"Swacharana vinivishtai........*
*.........mastit tatra chitram kalanch."*

In all these examples there is a 'beat', a tune, a tone with a thud, which sings very easily. When a reader reads this poetry, his position is just like a person, who dances with the tune or the tone of the poetry - may he know the meaning or not - but yet and still, he feels attuned with the rhyme, rhythm, and cadence of the poetry:

*'Talishu Talam, Vitapeshu Mandram........*
*...........Talanusarren Patanti Dhara."*

*(Mruchhakatik - 5/52)*

The rain drops when they fall on the Palm trees, they drop with high noise, on the trees with a sonorous sound, on the stones with harshness, and on the water, with a peculiar sound and thus the rain falls - but it does weave a tune like a 'vina-swar'. In this the falling water streams are compared with the Musical instrument, and at the time of reading, the reader, without under-standing the meaning, falls in line with the tune of the poetry. One more example from Uttar Ramcharita 4.29.

*"Jyajivahya valayitotkatkotirdrashta.........*
*........... vikatodarmastu chapam..........."*

According to Indian poetry, at times, the poets create such formations of sentences; the use of words, that according to stylistics, the writer intends to create an impact on the mind of the reader, that when the reader, reads, he feels that some strong and unusual scene is going to take place.

2. When one reads a poem, he tries to understand the meaning step by step and in the end, he feels the tune according to the meaning.

e.g.

*'Tato Mrugendrasya Mrugendragami Vadhay vadhyasya sharam Sharanyah"*
*Jatabhishango Nrupati...... Prasambodhrutarih."*

*(Raghuvnsh. 2/30)*

The king advanced towards the Lion; he was destroyer of the enemies, and in order to kill the lion, he tried to take out the arrow from its pad". When the reader reads, he gets the hint that the King, is going to kill the lion, howsoever strong the latter be. The reader moves with King Dilip and gets satisfaction at the bravery of the king and his spirit.

*"Tara Radanam Vadanasya Chandram,...........*
*Mahibhujah kasya na bhojayantiam........... Naishadh. 10.107"*

The beauty of the teeth of Damayanti has won the stars, the beauty of the face has won the moon, and the beauty of the hair has won the sky - thus which king is not satisfied with her beauty ? At the time of the reading of the poem itself, one gets the idea of the poet's mind.

In this context, it is necessary to mention that the speed of the poetry is dependent on the combination of the sentences and its dependence on one another and if it is not there, there will be lack of rhyme and meter composition. For the poetic taste it is called 'perfection of words' and then only it is called a poetry; if there is no union of both, it can not be called poetry, although it may be in a poetical form. Shushkah vriksha tishtai agre" and 'puratah nirasataru vilasati' are the examples of what is stated above.

**YATI** - Pause or break - at an interval. When the poetry is composed according to rules of the meters, in any language, in Sanskrit or English there is a pause at a particular stage, where a break, in speaking, listening, singing, rhyming, etc. so that, the speaker and the reader both can enjoy the meaning of the poetry. In some, there are 3 or sometimes there are 5 pauses - breaks according to the context of the poetry. Poetry is based on rules and regulations and not at random. For example,

(a) *How pleasant/to know/Mr. Lear !*
*Who has written/such volume of stuff !*

*(b) John Gilpin/was a citizen/of credit/and renown.*

*(Linguistics P. 35)*

In construction of any poetry, this sort of break or pause, gives charm to the poetry and it is on account of the stop/break/pause, that it becomes easy to follow the meaning of the poetry, howsoever difficultyful the composition may be. Before we complete the poetry, the pause gives us an idea about the whole poetry at once, without having completed it in to.

When you listen to 'Shardulvikridit' Chhanda, at once you will feel a feeling of 'Vira Rasa'. On listening Mandakranta, one feels either 'Karuna Rasa' or 'Shringar Rasa' and 'Dodhak' Chhanda makes you laugh - it creates 'Hasya Rasa'. 'Panch-Chamar' are the chhandas which are related to harder feelings, where as 'Malini', Sragdhara', etc. they are soft chhandas. In Vruta Ranatakar - 136 and 127 - are two examples of Shardulvikridit and Mandakaranta Chhanda, which are specimen of these expressions and feelings.

Thus to come to the conclusion, in Sanskrit Poetry, the main dependency is on the movement (Gati) - tone - tune; but then there is a pause, a stop a break at a particular level in larger metered chhandas and not in small, because there is no possibility of a break. There are rules that the letters in each line or half-line, should be according to rules only, otherwise, there would be breakage of rules, which would not be allowed in poetical composition of a particular type - say in a peculiar chhanda. Anushtap has to be 8 letters in each 'Pada'; and if there more than 8 letters, it is not 'Anushtap' chhanda. The same is the case with the rest of the Chhandas - there are rules especially made for this composition; A particular chhanda has to be with a particular number of letters, with a pause at a particular level - these are set rules - unchangeable; If any poet or a composer breaks the rule and tries to compose according to his caprice, it is his good luck; It cannot be good poetry - but a composition composed at sweet will, carrying no brand name of a chhanda. There is a chhanda Shashtra for this.

According to Sanskrit Kavya Shashtra, these chhandas are branded into 3 different categories; 1. Samavrutta, 2. Ardha Samavrutta, and 3. Visham vrutta. All these have formations - light and heavy - according to the stress according to meters of chhandas - these are long and tedious narration, which does not totally relate to our 'subject' and hence we shall summarise only. These Chhandas are singable also; they can be sung in special 'Ragas', according to 'tala' - tone and tune. It is a long story.

**4. RHYME**

How we touch the topic of rhyme:

'Once a rhyme scheme is established in a poem or in a poetic tradition, the hearer expects a recurrence of sounds, but he does not know which exact word will provide the chime. A poor poet slips into expected rhymes, until, as Pope put it; 'Where-e' er you find......'

*(Stylistics p. 65)*

A better poet finds words less frequently yoked in rhyme, perhaps different parts of speech or words of different grammatical composition. As discussed heretofore, in Indian poetics, there is importance of number of letters, and the sentences; and similarly there is equal importance of 'rhyme' too. When a poet used the word 'breeze', the corresponding word 'trees' is not far behind; when there is a word 'creep', the word 'sleep' is not far behind. This has been commented upon by Pope in his book e.g.

*"Where-e'er you find 'the western breeze',*
*In the next line 'whispers thro' the trees',*

*"If crystal streams' with pleasing murmurs creep'*
*The reader's threaten'd (not in vain) with 'sleep'*

*(Stylistics p. 65)*

But opposite to it, a good poet does not depend on rhyme, but if at all he uses them, he uses different forms of grammar in a different way. For example, Adrian Mitchele in his following lines, uses the words like Kate's, states, bills, thrills, Yeats, -

*'My girl kate's teaching in the States,*
*Lecturing from town to town,*
*Pays her bills by, gets her thrills by*
*Studying the influence of Yeats on Yeats on yeats.'*

*(Linguistics and Literature p. 65)*

The rhyme is used weather in the first half and then in the second half; or in the 2nd and 4th lines of a poetry. Some times the rhyme is only in 2nd and 4th lines. In Sahitya Darpana, in Kavyaprakasha, in Geet Govind, there are many examples in Sanskrit Languages, about the rhyme at every stage; there is no shloka without rhyme practically so to say. Sanskrit pandits have gone deep into details at every small step and formed rules and regulations as to how rhyme should be weaved; but then right from Rigved to present day poets, they may or may not resort to rhyme at all. In Sanskrit language the words used in a Shloka, are themselves form one sort of rhyme - one word with the another, one sentence with the other, and while reading the poetry itself, one comes across the meaning thereof very clearly. But does that mean that others are more important and these are less - no that is not the case. The tune is the embellishment of the poetry and the rhyme is the touch for its rise in the field - but both help the poet in formation of the poetry; If the rhyme is there, well and good, and by chance if it is not there, it is also well and good.

**Non-Contextuality**

Now we shall direct our attention to one more division of the Stylistics, which embellishes the poetic formula. According to Indian poetics, for comparison - one with the other - there are four divisions to asses the comparison - (1) Upameya - This is called Tenor - T - Upaman - The vehicle (V) and 'Saman Dharma' - Common ground - (C) In Indian philosophy the 4th one is 'Vahak Shabda - where as in English it is not taken into consideration. According to stylistics, in the criticism of any poetry, we have to refer to 'Prastut' (Upameya) and 'Aprastut' (Upaman) and reference of one for the another is called non-contextuality - Aprastut-vidhan. According to Indian Poetics, the main embellishment in a poetry is 'Comparison' - it is the main embellishment/ornament of the poetry. Then the critics have made two divisions further:

1. Rachana-parak Aprastut Vidhan.
2. Bimbparak Aprastut Vidhan.

In Sanskrit language in Sahitya Darpana 10-11, there is a good example of this. Similarly for 'Pada-Shlesh', Nalchampu 106, gives another example on this subject. However there are 8 divisions, according to grammar - Varna, Pratyay, Ling, Prakruti, Pada, Vibhakti Vachan or Bhasha. There are many examples on the subject, but for want of space and time we just omit them - we give only one example from English literature;

*"And when he rode, men myghte his braydel here.*
*Gyngen in whistlynge wynd also cleere,*
*And eek as loude as looth the chaple belle."*

*(G. Chaucer, General Prologue 169-171, Stylistics p. 133)*

One more -

*Thy soul was like a star and dwelt apart,*
*Thou hadst a voice whose sound was like the sea"*

*(Wordsworth: London, 1802)*

Still one more:

*Old as a coat on a hair and his crushed hand*
*as unexpressive as a bird's face.*

*(Terrence Tiller: Egyptian Beggar)*

*He trod the line*
*Like a buck in spring.I have seen old ships sail like swan asleep.*

*(J.E. Flecker: 'Theold Ships')*

Thick as autumnal leaves (Milton, 'Paradise Lost. Bk.1.)

Metaphor - Example -

*"I feed a flame within which so torments me*
*That it both pains my heart and yet contents me.'*

*(Dryden: 'Hidden Flame')*

Shakespeare's 'Julius Ceaser' - Antony -

*Put a tongue*
*In every wound of Caesar, that should move*
*The stones of poem to rise and mutiny"*

*(Julius Caeser III.II)*

*If music be the food of love, play on*

*(Shakespeare: Twelfth Night I)*

*So I unto myself alone with sing;*
*The woods shall to me answer and my echo ring.*

*(Spencer: Epithalamion)*

More from Milton:

*And cause the golden - tressed sun*
*All the day long his course to run.*

One type of sensory perception is expressed in terms of another and a Non-human reference is given human attributes. A terrible beauty is born (W.B. Years: Easter 1916). Some books are to be tasted, others to be swallowed, and some few to be chewed and digested. (Bacon: 'Of studies)

An abstraction is treated as if it were animate.

*A resort to Exaggeration:*
*Desolate and lone*
*All night long on the lake*
*Where fog trains and mist creeps,*
*The while of the boar,*
*Calls and cries unendingly*
*Like some lost child*
*In tears and trouble*
*Hunting the harbor's breast*
*and the harbor's eyes.*

*(Carl Sandburg: Lost)*

*Fair stood the wind for France,*
*When we our sails advance.*

*(Michael Drayton: Againcourt)*

*Lay your sleeping head, my love,*
*Human on my faithless arm.*

Westerners have given one more classification - Meiosis - where by negation, there is an air of appreciation. Meiosis is conscious understatement, with its special type litotes which uses negative construction to foreground an intended positive emphasis. (Linguistics and Literature p. 78)

*A thing of beauty is a joy for ever,*
*Its loveliness increases; it will never*
*Pass into nothingness.*

*(Keats: Endymion')*

According to Indian poetics, 'Vyangarth' has also a beauty in the 'Vastu Dhwani', wherein the positive is turned into negative and vice versa. This is a specimen of 'Meiosis', which according to Indian version comes into 'Upanhuti Alankar', which creates sensation in the poetry.

> *Neyam Nabhomandalmanburashi, Taitascha tara navafenbhanga,*
> *Nayam shahsi kundalitah fanindra, Nasau Kalankah shayi to Murari."*

*(Sa.Da. 10. 39)*

This is not Sky - this is ocean; these are not stars - these are the pieces of oasis. This is not the moon, it is Sheshanaga hitting in a pose; This is not spot on the moon; it is Lord Vishnu sleeping on Sheshanaga. These sort of Non-contextual versions are many in Sanskrit Literature;

> *e.g. Sancharini Dipashikheva Ratro, yam yam vyatiyay pativara sa,*
> *Narendra margatta eve prapede vivarnabhavam sa sa bhumipalah.*

*(Raghuvansh - 6.67)*

The specimen is excellent. Indumati is compared to a lamp-let, passing on the road, and when she passes the light falls on the face of the kings and when she moves, the light gets out. Again,

> *Gnane maunam Khashama Shaktau Nyage Shlaghaviparyayah,*
> *Gunah Gunanubandhitatat tasya saprasava eve.*

*(Raghuvansha. 1. 22)*

This is about King Dilip giving description about his qualities. There are many examples in Sanskrit literature, which are countless in number; There are about 10 divisions of Upma Alankar and specimen of each will take quite some time and space.

**CHOICE**

The last factor in Stylistics is 'Choice' or to be very precise 'Selection of a word, a phrase a sentence to give stress to the meaning.

There are about 10 synonyms, but the choice or the selection of a particular word conveys and carries the meaning of the word, which the writer desires to convey. The choice word stress the point to the heart. No other word could be used at that particular place.

A respected literary style is one, in which each of vocabulary or grammar is arrived at by exercise of the writer's Judgment and sensibility.

*(A Linguistic guide to English Poetry. p. 27)*

This is confirmed by the following example :

*'Dwayam Gatam Samparti Shoniyatam........*
*.........Lokasya cha tetra kaumudi."*

*(Ku.Sam.5.71)*

Here the stress on the word 'Kapali' used by the poet - there are many names of God Shankara, the selection, the choice of the word 'Kapali' is carrying the meaning, which is desired to be conveyed.

Further -

*"The blood-dimmed tide is loosed and everywhere*
*The ceremony of innocence is drowned.*

*(Yeats: The Second coming)*

The use of the word 'tide' with 'Drowned' is most appropriate. 'innocence' is significative as also the word 'ceremony' is impressive.

*Ten thousand saw I at a glance*
*Tossing their heads in sprightly dance.*

*(Wordsworth - daffodils)*

The word 'sprightly' carries the correct meaning. Further -

*A man so various, that he seemed to be*
*Not one, but all mankind's epitome*

*(Dryden; 'Alsalom and achitophel')*

The word 'various' is significative, - it does not relate to one man, but to entire mankind:

In the Drama of Shakespeare - in Hamlet - Hemlet accuses his uncle Claudius about the murder of his father - and he says-

*A Cutpurse of the empire and the rule,*

*that from a shelf the precious daidem stole,*
*and put it in his pocket.*

*(Hamlet III. IV)*

The words expressed are so impressive that it appears that these words have come out spontaneously - the alliteration of word 'p' at various places put force in the expression.

Hemlet's indictment of Claudius approaches its climax with lines that sound as if they were spat out of a mouth tense with fury. The plosives and harsh consonants clusters are grouped mostly around short close or half-close vowels in a way that suggests the Physiological result of inner tension. Through the whole utterance, the letter 'p' sound recurs with the contemptuous blowing of the lips that eventually underlines the sneer of the colloquial sneaing phrase ('Put it in his pocket' (ibid p. 39).

Thus by selection of letters, words, sentences, the writer has shown his talent in giving us a picturesque scene before us - even if you read these words, the drama is being enacted before your own eyes. It is so impressive, expressive, thought-provoking that it beggars description. The hemlet's speech towards Claudius is full of hate, disgust, insult, hatred and scorn - as if he is talking to a Hamlet's lips, perspiration drizzling from the brows, hot nose-end, having breath, fierce face, eyes red with anger, - all picture is before us a scene incarnate. This has happened only due to the choice of best words and expression.

The selection of the words should be done taking into consideration of the personality of the speaker - who speaks, when, how and at what stage, - all these combination make the best picture. Now we take an example of Wordsworth, where a five/seven year old boy gives us a description about the rainy season:

*By night or day*
*The things which I have seen I now can see no more.*
*The rainbow comes and goes*
*And lovely is the rose.*

*(Wordsworth: Immortality Ode)*

Now let us take another example by 'Black', where he too makes a 8/10 year boy speak few lines, which gives full meaning, which the poet desires to convey, but they do not appear to have been spoken of the boy of that age; these words are mature words, with mature thinking, and thus it creates an anomaly of understanding:

*My mother groaned, my father wept*
*Into the dangerous would I leapt*
*Helpless naked, piping loud,*
*Like a fiend hid in a cloud.*

*(Linguistics and Literature p. 39)*

The speech must be in conformity of the speaker's age, environment, embllishment; according to Anandvardhan, the 'Nayak' - the Hero' should be categorised - Dhiro taddtt, Dhirodhatt, Dhir lalit, Dhir prashant. Here we shall have cursary look at Uttar Ram Charitam Wherein Lava Kusha - at the time of battle- field dialogue - speaks words to Chandraketu, against and about Rama which are unworthy, although they might have been written by an eminent writer like Bhavabhuti. A boy of 12 speaks as if a man of 32 speaks and that also in waste-language; running down a chief character of Ramayana. Thus to be precise, the choice of words requires great care and concern, whosoever, howsoever one big may be.

Then there is a prohibition of using 'village-colloquial words', which are commonly spoken in the villages, but on the stage, such expression is not welcome; may be the writer want to introduce laughter or a lighter situation, but still one has to a be wary. It is also unwhole some, when a man speaks his speech with a mouthfull of 'bettle-nut' and 'tobacco'; of course, in villages these do happen, but not in the books of literature or on the stage - but then it is admitted that the particular situation at a particular place does deserve such inclusion; Not only that but indecent words, in whatever form, are also not allowed; there are some words which have double meaning - good as well as bad and as such, such usage is out of taste in higher class societies. But then there are exceptions also. When the word 'Subhaga' is used, we do not discuss about the 'vagina', nor when we use the word 'Abhipret', we discuss about a Pret' - a ghost. When we speak of "Shiva-ling', we do not discuss about any 'Phallus', but the word combined carries reverence towards Lord God Shiva.

*I saw a lily on thy brow*
*With anguish moist, and fever dew*

*(Keats: 'La Belle Dame Sans Merci')*

Here by the word 'Lily' drives at the purity of the beloved and the anguish moist. The use of words 'fever dew' is also significative.

According to Sanskrit literature, the choice of the words is covered by six points and they are 'Lakshgyata', 'Abhyas', 'Vruddhsewa', Avekshan', 'Pratibha' and 'Avadhan'.

According to Ka.Su. Vru. 1.3.15, it manifests that the choice of the appropriate words make the poet perfect. According to Bhamah, a poet has to select the choice words just like weaving a flower garland. (Kavyalankar - Bhamah 1.59).

Anandvardhan touches the Vyangarth (Dhwani) and he manifests that the poet should know the word and then use it. (Dhwanyalok 1.8) After Anandvardhan, Kuntak has also emphasised on the selection of words (Vakrokti Jivitam 1.7 and 1.9) wherein he has thrown sufficient light on the selection of words.

*Others too say the same thing :*
*'Shabdartho Sahitau Kavyam - Bhamah,*
*Nanu Shabdartho Kavyam - Rudrat*
*Shabdartho Sahitau Vakra Kavi Vyapar - Kuntak,*
*Taddaushau shabdartho sagaunau - Mammat.*
*Sahityamanayoh Shobha Shalitam prati kapyasau,*

*(Vakr. Jivi. 1.7)*

*Hridaye Vasisiti Matpriyam.....*
*.......Anangh Kathamkshata Ratihi. (Kumar Sambhav. 4.9)*
*Panth Natra Srastaramasti..........*

*(Sahitya. Darp. 4.6)*

In all these shlokas the selection of words is the main choice. Similarly we may quote one more to emphasise:

*"Alam Mahipal tav shramen.........*
*..........Shilochhaye Murchati Marutasya.*

*(Raghuvamsh 2.34)*

*Similarly in Ratnavali Natika, read about Sagarika:*

*'Parimlanam pinstanjaghansangadubhayatah,*

..........

..........

*Krushangyah santapam vadati bisinipatrashayanam.......*

*(Ratnavali 2.13)*

This gives full description of the body of the lady, because of the fact that a certain portion of the bed pressed/impressed, other is not and that shows her body structure; this could be arrived at, only by selection of choice words.

Choice of words go a long way in the Indian Sanskrit poetic field. The selection should be the selection - the word is used only to convey a particular meaning, which meaning is the only meaning fitted and appropriate - no other word - synonym - could replace the original word - replacement would be ridiculous. The poet's force in selection of first word is finale - the replacement would mar the meaning and would not convey the force which the first word has had; Thus the choice in poetic composition is of utmost value - it was yesterday - it is to-day, and it will remain so in future also; that is the beauty of the Indian poetic expression.

**Vakrokti Jivitam - by Kuntak**

In the previous pages, we have already at length about

1. Tillyard and his Oblique poetry.
2. Stylistics and Indian Poetry.

And now we shall take up the subject matter of 'Vakrokti Jivitam' by Kuntak and discuss further the delicacies of the topic.

Let us now refer to Sushil Kumar De's work on Kuntaka and summarise his views :

**Meaning of the Term Vakrokti**

In order to understand Kuntaka's peculiar idea of Vakrokti which underlies his theory of poetry, it will be necessary to trace the development of this idea in earlier and later Alamkara literature. A remarkable divergence of conception and treatment is noticeable in the theory of the Vakrokti held respectively by Bhamaha and Dandin, as well as Vamana, take the Vakrokti to imply something essentially different from the verbal poetic figure (Sabdaalmkara) of the same name defined and illustrated for the first time in Alamkara literature by Rudrata. According to him, the Vakrokti is a mere poetic figure

(Kavyalamkara) based upon a play on words and occurs as a kind of pretended speech, in which a sentence or word spoken in one sense by a speaker is taken in another sense by another speaker, either because it may be uttered with a peculiar intotation (Kaku), which changes its meaning or because, it may be supposed to admit of a double meaning (slesha), the object of this intentional mistake being that of making a suitable or clever reply. It consists, therefore, essentially in a deliberate misunderstanding of one's word for the purpose of making an ingenious retort, and is based on concealment (apahanava), on the understanding of a secret sense (gudharthapratiti). This Vakrokti is illustrated in the latter part of the 9th century by Rathnakara in his Vakrokti panchasika, but it is probably not the same term used in Raghava- Pandaviya. Where Kaviraja speaks of subandhu, Bhanabhatta and himself as poets who are skilled in the use of Vakrokti. At any rate, it appears as such in all theorists from Rudrata's time, who accept this interpretation as authoritative; and the older and broader connotation of the term seems to have been entirely lost from that date.

This older connotation appears in three distinct aspects in Bhamaha, Dandin and Vamana respectively. Bhamaha, who does not appear to put much store by such artificial tricks, means by vakrokti, something other than an excellence of composition (guna) or a mere poetic figure (alankara) such as we find it in later writers who follow Rudrata. The theoretical distinction between Guna and Alankara as such was of no great importance to Bhamaha; and though Bhamaha speaks of Vakrokti in connection with the figure atisayokti, the significance of which we shall explain presently, he does not yet regard Vakrokti as a poetic figure.

In his Kavyalamkara Ch. I. Bhamaha, in connection with his classification of the different species of Kavya, says that the subdivisions of Poetry mentioned by him are admissible to the designation of a Kavya in so far as they possess Vakrokti (I. 30); and this is made more clear by declaring later on that the Vakrokti is desirable for the purpose of adorning poetic speech (i. 36; v. 66), which he characterises elsewhere as Vakra (vi. 23). After defining and illustrating among other figures, the figure atisayokti Bhamaha declares saisa sarvaiva Vakrokti, apparently identifying thereby the atisayokti with what appears as the traditional Vakrokti, which he has not defined indeed but which he has already alluded to as a necessary element of Poetry. It also appears that although the Vakrokti is identified in substance with that figure atisayokti, it is yet not regarded as a special alamkara. This is clear not only from Kuntaka's later elaboration of the same idea and Bhatti's omission of Vakrokti from his illustration of poetic figures, but also from Bhamaha's own indication in the context; for Bahamas rejects (as also Kuntaka) the figure hetu, suksma, and lesa (accepted by Dandin) as poetic genius, inasmuch as they do not involve vakrokti (ii. 86). If he had taken Vakrokti as an independent poetic figure, then all the figures which involve Vakrokti (and Bhamaha thinks all figures should involve Vakrokti element) would constitute mixed alamkara. No alamkar however, is mixed in his opinion simply because it contains vakrokti; for which vakrokti in such cases apparently forms an essential part of the figure in which it is involved.

It seems, therefore, that Bhamaha regards Vakrokti not as an alamkara but as a characteristic mode of expression which underlies all alamkars and which thus forms an essential element of Poetry itself, whose meaning can be manifested by vakrokti alone; for Bhamaha lays down (ii. 85).

*Saisa sarvaiva vakrokti anayartho vibhavyate*
*yatno'sayam kavina karyah ok'lamkaro'naya vina.*

What is a poetic figure without vakrokti ? He characteristically asks; and as he lays down elsewhere that the vakrokti must be present in various kinds of poetic effort like the mahakavya, nataka, katha and akhayayika, as well as underlie a poetic figure as its essential mark, it is no wonder that the should regard vakrokti as primarily manifesting the sense of poetry and call upon the poet to be diligent with respect to it.

Thus, the vakrokti is taken by Bhamaha as the fundamental principle of all figurative expression, and indirectly of Poetry itself. In identifying it with the atisayokti Bhamaha partly implies that the lokatikranta-gocharam vacah, which is given as the essential characteristic of that figures (ii. 81) is also a characteristic of his Vakrokti as a mode of expression. The vakrata, explained by Abhinavagupta (Lochana p. 208) as Lokottirnena rupenavasthanan, implies a heightened form of expression different from matter-of-fact speech and involved in all figurative of poetic expression. Bhamaha probably means to imply that the Vakrata, resulting in a kind of atisayokti, is a certain charmingness of expression or rather imaginativeness which is necessary to constitute a poetic figure, and which is absent in common speech where facts are simply stated. When words are used in the ordinary manner, as people without a poetic turn of mind use them, there is no charm, no strikingness, no vakrata and consequently they are not poetical as Bhamaha understands it; they are merely what some writers woulds call vratta (ii. 87). Such swabhavokti or natural mode of speech, to which Dandin is so partial, is not acceptable to Bhamaha who refuses to acknowledge swabhavokti as a poetic figure at all. It is only when words are used in a charming sense or in an extraordinary manner that we have what we call a poetic figure and true poetry.

Dandin, however, limits and scope of vakrokti in so far as he distinguishes it from swabhavokti and used the term as a collective designation for all alamkaras (alamkara-samanya- vachana as Ruyyaka puts it) with the exception that the latter figure. In his Kavyadarsa ii which deals with the characteristics of different poetic figures, Dandin brings (ii. 8) by defining swabhavokti as the adya alamkrtih or the first or primary poetic figure. Then after dealing with other independent figures, he goes on to discuss in ii. 358-62 why he does not accept the claims of ananvaya, sasamdeha, upama-rupaka and utpreksavayava as independent figures. After this he speaks of samassti or samkirna. Then comes the important verse (ii. 362 in which alone he speaks of vakrokti:

*Slesah sarvasu pusnati pryo vakroktisu sriyam*
*dvidha bhinnam svabhavokit vakroktis ceti vanmayam.*

From this verse it appears at first sight that Dandin is in complete agreement with Bhamaha, but in differing from him in so far as he distinguishes swabhavokti from vakrokti, dividing all poetical speech into these two modes. But from the context as well as from Dandin's general treatment, it will appear that although Dandin means substantially the same thing, he implies by the term vakrokti only a collective name for all poetic figures, excepting the 'first' or 'primary' figure svabhavokti. For, after having spoken of mixed figures, Dandin in the verse cited says that slesa, itself a figure, produces charm in all poetic figures; and from this point of view all alamkaras (excepting svabhavokti in which indeed there is no scope for slesa) may be regarded as Samkirna. The verse under discussion, therefore, comes in quite pertinently in connection with samkirna figures, with the remark that slesa comes in almost all poetic figures. The verse, therefore, may be roughly translated thus 'Poetical speech is divided into svabhavokti and all other figures (collectively called Vakrokti); in the latter case, generally speaking, slesa unfurls its beauty. Dandin thus uses the term vakrokti in a somewhat restricted sense from that of Bhamaha, modifying it and confirming it into the more definite significance of a collective designation of the poetic figures in general. That this is meant by Dandin is clear from two old commentaries given in the Madras edition of the text. The Hrdayangama commentary thus explains the verse; slesa na kevalam arthantaranyasa eva sarvasu vakroktisvapi sriyam janayati! vanmayasya dvaividhyam darsayati bhinnam it! svabhavoktir adyalamkarah vakrokti sabden-upamadayah samkirna-paryanta alankara uchyante. Taruna vachaspati agrees with this interpretation, but differs as to what group of alamkaras Dandin signifies by this collective name; svavyakhyana-vyatirikta serva slamkritir vakroktir iti uchyate. It may be remarked, however, that apart from technical considerations, the distinction implied here is practically (as Kuntak) as treatment would shew a distinction without a difference; and Dandin's use of the term may betake for all practical purposes, to be nearly the same as Bhamahs.

Vamana, however, uses the term vakrokti in an entirely different sense. He was the first to apply it to designate a special poetic figure; but he differs from Rudrata in applying it to the case of an arthalankara and gives it a more or less general commutation to indicate a particular mode of metaphorical expression based on Laksana. This arthalamkara, according to him, occurs where the indicated sense (laksana) is based on the idea of similarity (sadrsya). It is thus, essentially a metaphorical mode of speech, and is distinct from the vakrokti of earlier writers.

An attempt has been made in the above exposition to demonstrate that while Bhamaha and Dandin use the term vakrokti in an extended and general sense, Vamana and Rudrata employ it to a designate a particular figure of speech, whether the figure be a sabdalamkara or an arthalamkara. While Rudrata's definition became standardised in latter literature, we find hardly any surviving trace of Dandin's and Vamanas' idea of the same. Bhamaha's vakrokti, however, found an exponent in Kuntaka who develops its implications fully in his vakrokti-jivitam and builds a unique theory of Poetics on its basis. He adopts Bhamaha's idea of vakrokti as the distinguishing characteristic of all poetic figures (alamkara-samanya-laksana) and employs it to denote selection of words and turning of ideas which are peculiar to poetry and which are abhorrent of matter-of-fact speech. But he analyses all poetic speech from this standpoint and elaborately develops what is only hinted at by Bhamaha.

**Kuntaka's theory of Poetry**

At the outset of his work, Kuntaka lays down briefly that his object in writing a fresh treatise on Poetics, when many others exist already in the field, is 'to establish the idea of vaichitrya which causes extraordinary or disinterested charm in poetry (lokottara-Chamat-kara-kari-vaichitriya-siddhaye). This pithy phrase, which sums up the characteristics of what he means by vakrokti in poetry, practically forms the central principal of his poetic theory. For the Vakrokti, which he maintains to be essential in poetry, is taken as a kind of vichitra-abhidha, so that the vakratva or vakra-bhava under lying it becomes synonymous with vichitraya or vichitra-bhava. Indeed, Kuntaka does not appear to make any distinction between them but uses them as interchangeable terms. This vakrata or vaichitrya is explained as sastradi-prasiddha-sabdarthopai bandhavyatereki, or more generally as prasiddha-prasthana-vyatireki, or atikranta prasiddha-vyavahara-sarani. In other words, it consists of a strikingness of expression which is different from the established or current mode of speech, such as we find in the sastras and the like. It is thus a deviation from the matter of fact manner of treatment established in the sciences and the scripture; or, more widely, from established usage in general. Mahimbhatta explains this standpoint clearly when he says that when contrary to established usage, an idea is expressed with a view to attain strikingness, we have what is called vakrokti.

Referring to the conventional definition that a word and its sense in their alliance constitute poetry, Kuntaka lays down the qualification that this alliance must have the speciality of being characterised by what he calls vakratva or vaichitrya. He does not hold with Dandin that mere word, however charming, or mere idea constitute poetry - na sabdasyaiva ramaniyata- visistasya kevalasya kavyatvam, napyarthasya); what makes them into poetry is the presence of the vaichitrya due to vakrokti, which is therefore the essence of poetic speech.

This Vakrokti is further described as vaidagdhyabhangibhaniti, which is explained in the vrtti as a mode of expression (bhaniti) depending on the peculiar turn (bhangi or vicchitti) given to it by the skill of the poet (Vaidagdhya or kavi-kaushala). Ultimate emphasis is, therefore, laid (as Ryaka also points out) on Kavi- Kaushala which is elsewhere designated more comprehensively as Kavi-vyapara or an act of the imagination of the part of the poet. The Vakra-kavi-vyapara or kavi-vyapara-vakrata is, in Kuntaka's opinion, the ultimate source of poetry. The Vakrokti is this a bhaniti-prakara, or in the terminology of Ruyaka an ukti- vaichitrya which rests entirely on the genius of the poet.

It follows from this exposition that Kuntaka like Bhamaha, cannot accept any composition involving mere svabhavokti, although Dandin and other have given prominence to this particular figure, which consists in a description of the natural disposition Svabhava) of an object. When we make use of an embellishment (alamkara), what we embellish is the svabhava of an object. If this svabhava itself is an embellishment, as it is in svabhavokti, what is there left to be embellished ? To Kuntaka, a plain description of this svabhava (as he takes it) is obviously without the requisite strikingness; and he is naturally afraid, apart from technical objection, that the inclusion of this figure would admit even common place unadorned expressions into poetry. But this does not mean that Kuntaka entirely rejects the possibility of embellishing the svabhava of an object. He includes it in the scope of a special kind of vakyavakrata in which the svabhava of an object, whether sahaja or aharya, forms the legitimate these for heightened expression, and allows it as one of the elements of the simpler sukumara-marga.

Kuntaka also appears to agree with Bhamaha that the atisaya, which is paraphrases in one place as prakasha-kasthadhiroha, is involved in vakrokti-vaichitrya; and he takes it as a necessary element in what he calls vichitra-marga. But as this vaichitrya, which consists in a departure from conventional usage (prasisdha- vyatireketva) may be attained by wild or eccentric writing, it is laid down that it should be tadvid-ahlada-kari or capable of pleasing the connoisseur. The tadvid-ahlada-karitva is defined as consisting of a pleasing enjoyment beyond what is afforded by the excellence of word, sense or embellishment. Thus the ultimate test of this vaichitrya in poetry is tadvid-ahlada or the appreciation of the sahrdays, the man of taste.

The tad-vid or sahrdaya plays an important part in poetic theories. The Sanskrit authors clearly assert every one is not capable of realising the charm of poetry (consisting of the vaichitrya, lokottara ahlada or chamatkara underlying rasa or vakrokti) and demand a degree of culture and aesthetic instinct in the capable reader, the rasika or the sa-hradaya. He is the expert who must not only be initiated into the intricacies of theoratic requirements (Kavyartha-vid) but must also possess the finer capacity of aesthetic enjoyment born out of wide culture and identification with the feelings and moods of the poet. Anandvardhan discusses sahrdayatva at some length at p. 160 and Abhinavagupta arrives at a concise definition of the sahrdaya thus. 'Yesham kavyanusilanabhyasavasad visadibhute mano-mukure varnaniya- tanmayi-bhavana-yogyata te hrdaya-samvadabhajah sahrdayah, a definition which became so much standardised that Hemachandra does not scruple to copy it literally.

Taking this broad connotation of Vakrokti, Kuntaka maintains that this vakrokti constitutes the only possible embellishment or alamkara of poetry. No doubt, for the sake of convenience of treatment, one speaks conventionally of alamkarya (that which is to be embellished, viz. the sabda and artha) and its alamakara (embellishment viz. the poetic figures); but this distinction, in his opinion, is not essential. The embellished speech itself in its entirely is poetry and the addition of poetic figures is not advantageous. His position appears to be that of embellished word and sense (alnkrata sabdartha) constitute poetry; and it is not proper to say that alamkaras belong to kavya, for this statement would suggest that kavya may exist without them. Indeed, Vakrokti as a mode of expression being essential in poetry, it underlies and forms the substance of all poetic figures so called. In a sense, therefore Kuntaka (like Dandin) uses the term vakrokti as almost co-extensive with the generatic term alamkara; and in one place he paraphrases vakrokti- vaichitriya as alamkara-vichitra-bhava and vakrokti as sakalamkara-samanya. Later writers make his clear when they explain that Kuntaka takes the alamkaras as abhidhana-prakara- visesa and that vakrokti is nothing more than alamkara - samanya- vachana or alamkara-samanya-lakshana. As such, therefore, the vakrokti is, as Kuntaka hold, the only alamkriti possible to sabda and artha; and all so-called poetic figures are but different aspects of the vakrokti. As a matter of fact Kuntaka includes the alamkaras in the province of Vakya-vakrata.

The vakrokti being the only alamkara admissible, all other alamkaras or poetic figures so analysed by other writers can be properly included in its comprehensive scope. Kuntaka is conscious of the fact that the Kavi-vyapara, which is the source of vakrokti, is in its nature underfinable; yet one can distinguish and classify its function into six different spheres. The vakratva, created by kavi-vyapara, may occur in the following cases; (1) in the arrangement of letters which is termed as varna-vinyasa-vakrata. In this may be included among other things, all matters which other writers would include in anuprasa and yamaka. In the substantive (Pratipadika) or the terminal (pratyaya) part of a word, called respectively pada-purvardha and pada-parardha (or pratyaya) vakrata. In the former are included peculiar uses of paryaya (synonym) rudhi (conventional words), upachara (fancied identification founded on resemblance) visesana (attributing words) samvrati (covert expressions) vrtti (samasa and taddhita affixes) bhava (root of words), linga (gender and kriya (verb). In the second group of words are dealt with the peculiar uses of kala (tense) karaka (case) samkhya (number), purusa (person) upgraha (voice) and particles and indeclinables. (4) In a sentence called vakya_vakrata. The Vakya-vakrata may be of indefinite varieties (bhidyate shaharradha), for it depends on the fertile fancy of the poet (Kavi-pratibhanam anantyadniyatatvam na sambhavati). In this section is included the treatment of all poetic figures embracing those figures (e.g. rasavat, preyas etc.) which, according to older writers, involve rasas as an accessory element. But which, according to Kuntaka, delineate the rasas principally. This is the subject matter to be discussed later. (5) In a particular topic (prakarana), called prakarana_vakrata. (6) In the composition as a whole, called prabandha-vakrata. The next chapter is devoted to a consideration of these two subjects. With the exception of the introductory portion of the first chapter which deals with general principles, the whole of the work is devoted to the definition, classification and illustration of these varieties of vakrata, which forms the different categoreis into which poetic speech is analysed. But Kuntaka himself admits that vakrata may be of infinite kinds, depending on the creative genius of individual poet.

Kuntaka appears to put much more stress on riti than his master Bhamaha does, and his treatment of gunas appertaining there to is much more elaborate. In this he was probably influenced by the traditions of the riti-school. He acknowledges three margas (a term used both by Dandin and vamana as equivalent to riti), and these correspond to the three ritis of Vamana and his followers. But he finds fault with the classification and momen-clature of ritis adopted by these exponents of the riti-theory. Kuntaka alludes to Dandin's twofold and vamana's three fold classification of ritis, but asserts that if ritis are to be named and differentiated as vaidarbhi, gaudi, etc. after different localities in which they are supposed to flourish, then one would be forced to admit infinite varities of ritis as there is infinite number of countries. In his opinion, a particular riti cannot be established as a desa-dharma; for it does not depend on particular regional characteristics, or special custom of a particular place, but on the peculiarities of sakti (power), vyutpatti (culture) and abhyasa (practise) of particular types of poets, which can never conform to mere geographical distribution. To classify ritis, again, into good, bad or indifferent (Uttama, adhama and Madhyama) and give them geographical names in futile; for the best kind of poetry alone, the uttama kavya, which appeals to the sensibilities of the sahrdaya is to be accepted, and there is no point in admitting or framing rules for the so- called madhyama and adhama ritis. In this arguments Kuntaka anticipates the objections put forward by Mammata and his followers against the riti-theory generally; but Kuntaka admits the riti to be a distinct place in his system, adopting however, a different basis of classification. In his opinion, the kavi- svabhava alone furnishes the criterion for kavi-prasthana-bheda; and the ritis are to be classified according to the essential difference in the Sakti, Vyutpatti and abhyasa of particular type of poet. One class of poets has special fitness for compositions characterised by saukumarya, while others prefer vaichitrya, these being the two extreme styles of composition. But there may bestill other poets who would like to steer a middle course, thus favouring a mixed style.

Broadly speaking, the chief distinction between the Sukumara and the vichitra marga seems to be that in the former the kavi- kausala is not aharya (adventitious or artificial) because of the prominence given to the svabhava of things, and consequently whatever ornamentation it possesses is effected with the least effort while in the vichitrabhava, predominates and poetic effort is subordinated to this object. In the sukumara style then a rural powers of the poet find an unhampered scope and result in a kind of heightened (satisaya) expression; while in the vichitra style the art is chiefly decorative, and through it bhaniti- vaichitrya attains a peculiar factitious charm. The dhwani (or pratiyamanata as it is called) is an element in both; but in the former the rasa becomes an anga of the delineation of svabhava, while in the latter the ornamentation is to be done in accordance with the under-lying motives of rasa (rasakuta). In Kuntaka's opinion, the vichitra marga, which is favoured by all good poets, is the more difficult of the two, demanding greater skill and maturity of treatment.

To the sukumara marga belong the excellences of madhurya (sweetness due to fewness of compounds), prasada (perspicuity), lavanya (beauty arising out of proper arrangement of letters and words) and abhijatya (smoothness). The vicitra marga is similarly characterised by four sets of excellences, which are designated by the same names but defined somewhat differently; viz. madhurya (compactness of skillful structure avoiding laxity), prasada (lucidity due to the use of expressive words and easy syntax), lavanya (beauty due to the arrangement of short and long syllables), and abhijatya (elevatedness which is neither too soft nor too hard). The Madhyama marg, which stands midway between these two styles, combines the excellences of both (ubhayatmaka). To these special characteristics Kuntaka adds auchitya and saubhagya as excellences common to the three margas. The auchitya, which as a characteristic emphasises the fitness of words and ideas, had been admitted by the Dhwani school chiefly in connection with rasa, and discussed generally in a separate treatise by Kshemendra; while the saubhagya is an excellence which arises out of the realisation of all the resource of a composition.

From the prominence thus given to the analysis of alamkara, it will be clear that Kuntaka could not put enough emphasis on rasa and bhava as elements of poetry. The rasa is dealt with topically in connection with the poetic figures of the different margas in which it is involved, as also in the treatment of prakarana- prabhandha-vakrata. Kuntaka admits the necessity of rasa, but regards its delineation apparently as a special kind of realising vakratva in a composition. He quotes with approval an antara- shloka which lays down-

*nirantara-rasoddhara-garbha-sauddarya-nirbharah*
*Girah Kavinam jivanti na katha-matram asritah.*

He admits that it is not the mere matter or plot but the beauty imparted to it by the continuous development of rasa which can make the words of a poet live, and in this he follows the dictum of Anandvardhana but as he had already accepted the essentiality of vakrokti, the rasa could be comprehended only as an element of vakrokti. It would appear that the theorists of the school to which Kuntaka belonged were indeed cognisant of that aesthetic delectableness which must be present in poetry and which is Sanskrit goes by the name of rasa, they could not yet harmonise it with their theory of Alamkara, except indirectly as an embellishment of the language or of sense. Thus in the figure rasavat, which was recognised by old Poetics (Bhamaha/Dandin) and which helped to smuggle in, as it were, the idea of rasa into their systems, the moods and feelings are roused not for their own sake but only to adorn the expressed thought. Kuntaka substantially follows this tradition, but as in the meantime the Dhvanikara and Anandvardhana had already worked out the importance of rasa and indicated its position as an essential element in poetry, he had to assign to rasa a definite place in his system, and could no longer regard and rasavat etc. as convenient figures of speech in which the rasas could be included.

While discussing the kind of vakya-vakrata in which the sva-parispanda or svabhava of an object forms the theme. Kuntaka gives directions as to how sentient objects can be described and made attractive through the proper development of sentiments like love. He appears to accepts the theory of Anandvardhana that the rasas cannot be sva-sabda-vachya and gently ridicules those writers (e.g. Udbhatta) who hold views to the contrary. In this connection he points out how charming results can be produced in poetry by nourishing rasas and bhavas and cites verses from the vikramorvasiya and Tapasa-vatsaraja as illustrations of vipralambha shrinagara and karuna rasa respectively. He also comments upon the resoddipana-samarthya of Kumara and Vikramorvasiya. Incidentally he considers in detail the claims of the so-called rasalamkaras (rasavat, preyas, urjasvin and samahita) to be included in the list of alamkaras, as they were done by older writers who comprehended all idea of rasa in these figures. Kuntaka could not regard them in the samelight as they were viewed by older theorists like Bhamaha and Dandin nor could he regard them with Anandvardhana as cases of gunibhutavyangya in which the suggested sense (here rasa) is subordinated to the expressed poetic figure. He maintains that like svabhavokti, they are not alamkaras, but almakarya; i.e. in these so-called poetic genius, the rasa is developed for its own sake and not merely as an embellishment of the expressed thought. He criticises severely the older views of Bhamaha, Dandin, Udbhatta and others, commenting in detail upon their definitions and illustrations, and holds that the rasavat is neither darsita-spastra- sringaradirasam, or rasasrayam, nor rasa-pesalam, but rasena vartate tulyam, and cites the verse upodha-ragena as its proper illustration. But he is at the same time careful in laying down; rasa-svabhavalamkaranam sarvesam kavi-kausalam eve jivitam, indicating thereby that even the rasavat, in which rasa is independently developed is only an aspect of vakrata depending on kavi-kausala. If not theoretically invulnerable, this view is interesting as indicating that the importance of rasa, first advocated in poetic theories by the Dhavanikara appears to have influenced thinkers belonging to other traditions of thought. The Dhavanikara attempted to reconcile the older idea of rasavatas involving the rasas secondarily by admitting it in his second division of poetry; but Kuntaka brushes aside all older views in this respect, and thinks that the case of rasavat should be considered as one in which the poet has an opportunity of creating a kind of Vakrokti in which the rasa supplies the principal charm.

Thus, Kuntaka, recognising the importance of rasa in poetry, had to allow it to form all element of the two kinds of style, the sukumara and the vicitra. He lays down in general terms that vicchitti is sarasatva-sampaducita. He also allows the rasas to play an important part in what he calls prabhandha and prakarana- vakrata, i.e. in vakrata occurring in the composition as a whole on in its constituent episodes. In a prakarana, for instance, the special kind of vakrata-vicchitti (or the ingenious and charming turns) introduced in the incidents of a traditional plot is justified in so far as it contributions to the development of rasas (evam esam mahakavi-prabandehesu prakarana-vakrata-vicchittih rasa-nisyandidi etc.). Sometimes the prakarana- vakrata may be such that the angi or dominant rasa is developed in a act of a drama (e.g. in vikramorvasiya iv) to a climax which it has never attained either before or after. Sometimes a single rasa like karuna is developed and sustained through the play with constant repetition of the theme, but the vakrokti is thereby not rendered tiresome because it is woven with new surprises and made brilliant with rasa and alamkara. In a prabandha, again, the angi rasa of the original story may be abandoned in favour of another rasa to impart new charm to the plot. Thus in the veni- samhara the dominant santa rasa of the Mahabharata is rejected in favour of vira rasa.

Similar remarks apply to Kuntaka's treatment of the element of dhavani in poetry. It is clear that Kuntaka, who admits not the essentiality of rasa or dhvani, but that of vakrokti, can comprehend them only in some aspects of vakrata. Ruyyaka explains that all ideas of dhvani are acknowledged by Kuntaka in the special form of Vakrokti, called upachara-vakrata, the peculiarity of his view consisting in this recognition of the concept of the 'suggested sense' and in the attempt to in corporate it in vakrokti. From Kuntaka's treatment of upachara-vakrata, it appears that the upachara-vakrata lies at the root of such pleasing fitures as rupaka and therefore of metaphorical expression generally; and that, generally speaking, the upachara consist of a supposed or fancied identification of two objects, however, distinct, on the basis even of the slightest resemblance. The term upachara, do doubt, is often used loosely as identical with laksana (indication of Transferred Sense); but the above interpretation agrees with the idea of upachara expounded by a majority of theorists, and is put conscisely by Visvanatha as 'the arrest of the apprehension of difference between two objects, absolutely distinct, by means of the greatness of their resemblance;' As such, therefore, it is admittedly involved in figures like rupaka (metaphore) and forms the basis of metaphorical expression in general. As an instance of upachara-vakrata Kuntaka cites the case of application to immaterial objects of words which denote material objects, as in the phrase 'particle of abuse.' The word 'particle' applicable to material objects in the sense of 'little' bears a pleasing charm to the Sahrdaya, when it is applied, through the analogy of 'littleness' to such immaterial objects as 'abuse'. This view of upachara agrees with that of the Nyaya-vartika, which explains it as a 'tatcchbhadasya tacchabdenabhidhanam upacharah.' Kuntaka's upachara would come under the comprehensive domain of transferred expression known as Laksana, and would be included by the writers of the Dhwani School in the province of Laksana-muladhavani or Suggestion based on Transference of indication.

The Vakroktijivita-kara, therefore, may be classed (together with Bhamaha, Dandin, Udbhatta, and Vamana) among those who hold (according to the classification of the Dhvanikara and Anandvardhana) that dhvani or Suggestion is bhakta; or, in other words, among those who maintain that the suggested sense is not the essence of poetry but is only a secondary element. Kuntaka acknowledges the concept of Dhvani but denies its independent existence as 'the souls of the poetry' by including it under various forms of vakrokti, especially in upachara vakrata. Harichand Shastri, is hardly accurate in stating that the system of vakrokti, as propounded by Kuntaka, is also known as the system of bhakti. The word bhakti or bhakta, as explained by Abhinavagupta, is almost synonymous with laksana or laksanika, and is therefore, a very comprehensive term to indicate generally the systems of all writers who regard dhvani as a secondary element (bhakta or gauna) in poetry. Kuntaka, therefore, in maintaining the primary importance of vakrokti and regarding dhvani as a secondary element included therein certainly belongs to this school; but the same remark applies also Bhamaha, Udbhatta, Dandin and Vamana of older Poetics who apparently include all ideas of dhvani in particular poetics figures like paryayokta etc. Thus we see that the doctrine of vakrokti (in relation to the theory of dhvani), as set forth by Kuntaka, is not synonymous with but is only a variety of bhakti-vada, which is included to by the dhvanikara in the first verse of his work, but which takes several forms, as Abhinavagupta points out, according as the tadatmya or tadrupya (identity, as in the case of a paryaya or synonym) laksana (i.e. vyavartaka-dharma or differentiating property) or Upalaksana (i.e. kadacitka- vyavartaka-dharma or an occasional mark) of laksana or Indication is posited with reference to the function of vyanjana or Suggestion. Harichand is inaccurate, therefore, in stating that the Vakroktijivita-kara was the creator of the system of bhakti; to put it accurately Kuntaka belonged to that school of opinion which maintained, among other things, that bhakti or laksana alone is sufficient to explain the existence of the suggested sense, which is thus assigned secondary place in his system as an element of poetry. This view is sometimes technically known as antarbhava-vada; and Jayaratha, commenting on Ruyyaka's remarks about our another expressly says; idanim yadyapyanyair asys (=dhvaneh) bhaktiyantarbhavam ukttam tad api darsyaitum aha.

But in spite of the opinions of Ruyyaka, vidhyadhara and Jayaratha, it appears that Kuntaka is more fully alive to the importance dhvani in poetry than they would make us believe, and assigns to it a larger part in his scheme of Poetics than allowing it to be comprehended in all its aspects in upachara- vakrata merely. At the very outset of his work he defines vachaka sabda and vachya artha comprehensively as including in its scope not only laksaka sabda and laksaya artha but also vyanjaka and vyanjaka and vyangya word and sense, thus expressly recognising the three vrittis, including vyanjana, in poetry. He acknowledges the element of dhvani in the skukumara marga but more explicitly in the vichitra marka. In the category of pada-vakrata, the dhvani is admitted not only in upachara-vakrata, but also in rudhi-vaichitray-vakrata and in paryaya-vakrata. In the case of upachara-vakrata the verse gaanam ch mattameham from Gaudavaho is cited as an illustration, but Anandvardhana quotes the same verse as an example of atyanta-tiraskarata-vachya dhvani (i.e. the case of suggestion where the expressed sense disappears entirely). Under rudhi-vaichitra-vakrata, Kuntaka cites Anandvardhana's verse tala jaamti guna, as well as snigdha-syamala-kanti-lipta, which Anandvardhana quotes as an example of arthantara-samkramita-vachya dhavani; (i.e. the case of suggestion where the expressed sense passes into another sense). Thus the two cases of Laksana-mula dhvani, recognised by the Dhvani school, are acknowledged by Kuntaka. The paryaya-vakrata, again, where words with a double meaning lead to the suggestion of a metaphor or simile is expressly states by Kuntaka to fall within the province of what is called sabda-sakti-mula dhvani. Thus Kuntaka admits most of the broad divisions of dhvani elaborated by the dhvani- theorists.

Again Kuntaka recognises pritiyamanata generally in those cases of vakya-vakrata where the svabhava of an object forms the theme and guardedly uses the term gocharatva instead of vachyatva, so as to include the possibility of vyangyatava (vachyatveneti noktam, vyangyatvenapi pratipadana-sambhavat). He thus clearly indicates that such descriptions are possible not only through express words but also through suggestive expressions. In other words, he accepts in a general sense what is known as vastu- dhvani. In some of the poetic figures, again, he admits pratiyamanata. He gives illustrations of the pratiyamanta rupaka and pratiyamana vyatireka, and attempts to include figures like nidarsana, parivratti, etc. in the scope of pratiyamana upama. In this way he appears to acknowledge alamkara-dhvani, as elsewhere he acknowledge rasa-dhavani and vastu-dhvani. In one passage, while discussing the figure parivartti, which he would consider to be alamkarya (and not an alamkara), he gives his opinion that this so-called figures is charming when it involves suggestion, and speaks categorically in this connection of the three forms of suggestion of vastu, alamkara and rasa recognised by dhvani school; vastu-matram, alamkarah, rasadayas ceti tritayopapatteh.

Indeed, Kuntaka belongs to that group of authors who, having flourished after Anandavardhana's time, do not deny the concept of dhvani, but try to explain it in terms of already recognised ideas. Like Mahimbhatta, who attempts to settle the process of Suggestion by the technical logical process of Inference, Kuntaka lived in the interval between Anandvardhana, who first championed the dhvani-theory and Mamata whose classical text book raised the theory to almost exclusive authority. Like Mahimbhatta again Kuntaka, as a follower of Bhamaha, Udbhata and the alamkara school, started a vigorous but short-lived reactionary movement which wanted to go back to the old position in a somewhat original way by an attempt to reconcile new ideas with the old. In this lies the historical importance of Kuntaka's work. But like the anumana-theory of Mahimbhatta, still again, Kuntaka's theory of Vakrokti never appears to have received liberal recognition in the hands later theorists, all of which since Mammata's time, accepted without question the dhavani-theory of Anandvardhana. If later writers refer to his Vakrokti, it is only to criticise and reject it; and in attempting to revive and extend Bhamaha's old theory in the face of the more widely received theory of the Dhavanikara and Anandvardhana, *Kuntaka was apparently fighting on behalf of a cause already doomed*.

# The Exit

In the comparative stylistic study of Tilliyard and Kuntak, we have dealt at length with the pros and cons of the problem of LITOTES/VAKROKTI/SLANT-SAYING/OBLIQUE-WRITING taking into consideration views of both the sides - Eastern as well as Western - Oriental and Occidental, and before we end, we must admit that the fact remains supreme that EAST IS EAST AND WEST IS WEST'.

We have dealt with at length in all these pages, we have given various quotations, expressions, examples from both the cultures and finally we have come to the conclusion that we may try to compare, but both - the Eastern and Western - have their own qualities. An attempt to compare both the civilization with one angle - with one foot-rule - one ideology, it would be difficult to do so, because so many apparent reasons.

Both the hemispheres have produced best of the writers, poets, etc. and each one has excelled in one's own effort, but the basic cultural difference would definitely remain aloof, there cannot be a comparison of these two.

In Eastern Culture, we have GURU PARAMPARA, MATRU-BHAKTI, PITRIBHAKTI, GURUKUL SYSTEM, regards and respects of elders, old old tradition, - and reflections of these cultural involvement do appear in our writings;

Whereas in Western Culture - We study History - there is absence of all the above points - they are conspicious by their absence: How now then there can be comparison of two Diametrically opposite cultures ? Our Pundits - past and present - have gone deep into Sanskrit Literature and evolved a system, a method, after a passage of number of years. There is a lofty tradition of going into details in all the aspects, may be religious, cultural, social, political, environmental, - at every step and stage, eastern culture have gone into finer details. For example, here we discuss about poetry - our poetic shastras are more scientific, more traditional, more devoted more serious, more analytical, than the Western world.

While we do appreciated the efforts of Western writers to touch the eastern culture, but they can touch the seam only and not only they cannot, but could not drink deep, the vast ocean of knowledge of Indian culture and tradition.

We do not run down - we appreciate; that is all.

We finally say only that East is East and West is West and the twine shall never meet.

In this our humble effort, we have tried our best to critically analysis both the systems, and tried to arrive at a conclusion - we have given examples from both but yet we are not satisfied; we do not desire to do unjustice; nor we would like to be prejudicial, or preferential to one to the detriment to the other, and yet we admit that no one is perfect - in our going through volumes/writings/compositions of many ancient and modern writers, Indian tradition is definitely, decidedly finer, subtler, scientific, and systematic, the deep delving out of qualities of each aspect do deserve kudos to all-.

The Science is perfect - and if there is any fault, material or otherwise, we invite open criticism and invite Sahriday's observations on this humble effort. Kuntak's criticism/observation/analysis is based on intricate delicacies discussed in the foregoing pages - we have tried to discuss in detail and at length about the origin and the end of Poetic Science.

We observe that the selection of the word 'Oblique' is in itself a mis-nomer: the correct nomenclature is 'Litotes'- meaning different meaning, other than the meant. The word Irony is nearing the meaning. Slant-saying is also somewhat palatable, but not oblique. Now, after passage of these many years, it is not possible to change the original observation now, but then this is our observation, towards the problem. What the critics on the subject have to say, we don't know.

# Select Bibiliography


**BOOKS IN SANSKRIT**

अग्नि पुराण — आनन्दाश्रम सिरीज, पूना १९९१
अभिनव गुप्त — अभिनवभारती, सं. एम. रामकृष्ण बड़ौदा, १९५६
अप्पयदीक्षित — वृत्तिवार्तिक सं.पं. शिवदत्त, बम्बई १९४०
आनन्दवर्द्धन — ध्वन्यालोक सं. पट्टाभिराय शास्त्री, वाराणसी १९४०
उद्भट — काव्यालंकार सार संग्रह सं. नारायणदास, पूना १९७५
कुन्तक — वक्रोक्तिजीवित सं. सुशील कुमार डे, कलकत्ता १९६१
गणेश — त्रयम्वक देशपाण्डे, भारतीय साहित्यशास्त्र, बम्बई, १९६०
दण्डी — काव्यादर्श, सं. रङ्गाचार्य शास्त्री, पूना, १९३८
भामह — काव्यालङ्कार चौखम्भा संस्कृत सिरीज, वाराणसी
भोजराज — सरस्वती कंठाभरण सं. केदारनाथ दुर्गाप्रसाद बम्बई
मम्मट — काव्यप्रकाश सं. चौखम्भा संस्कृत सिरीज, वाराणसी
महिमभट्ट — व्यक्तिविवेक सं. मधुसूदन मिश्र, वाराणसी, १९३६
राजशेखर — काव्यमीमांसा चौखम्भा संस्कृत सिरीज, वाराणसी
रूय्यक — अलंकार सर्वस्व सं. गिरिजा प्रसाद द्विवेदी, बम्बई १९३६
रूद्रट — काव्यालंकार, सं. पण्डित दुर्गाप्रसाद , बम्बई, १९७८
विश्वनाथ — साहित्य दर्पण सं. शालग्रामशास्त्री, दिल्ली, १९५६
मुकुलभट्ट — अभिधा वृत्ति मातृका, निर्णय सागर प्रेस, बम्बई १९६४
वामन — काव्यालंकार सूत्र वृत्तिः, आत्माराम एण्डसंसए दिल्ली १९५४
पण्डितराज जगन्नाथ — रसगंगाधर निर्णयसागर प्रेस, बम्बई १९४७
अच्युतराय — साहित्यसार, निर्णयसागर प्रेश, बम्बई, १९०६
चन्द्रालोक — जगदेव, चौखम्भा संस्करण, १९३८

**BOOKS IN HINDI**

अरस्तू का काव्यशास्त्र — सं. डा. नग्रन्द्र प्र. सं. दिल्ली
चिन्तामणि — आचार्य रामचन्द्र शुक्ल, इंडियन प्रेस, प्रयाग

भारतीय काव्यसिद्धान्त — सं. काका कालेल कर एवं नगेद्र, दिल्ली

शैली विज्ञान की रूपरेखा — संधीय प्रकाशन, जयपुर

शैली विज्ञान — डॉ नगेन्द्र, नेशनल पब्लिशिंग हाउस, दिल्ली

रीति विज्ञान — विद्यानिवास मिश्र, राधाकृष्ण प्रकाशन, दिल्ली

**BOOKS IN ENGLISH**

E.M.W. Tillyard Poetry Direct and Oblique, London 1st Edition-1934.

Chapman Raymond; Linguistics and Literature Littlefield Adams

Chatman's and Levin, S.R. (eds.) 'Essays on the Language of Literature: Houghton Mifflin Boston.

Turner, G.W. Stylistics: Penguin.

G. Saintsbury, A History of English Criticism 1911.

Edwin Muir; The Estate of Poetry, Hegarth Press, London, 1962.

# Index to the Text